DIRK BOGARDE

Dirk Bogarde in *The Blue Lamp* 1950.

Dirk Bogarde in *Death in Venice* 1971.

DIRK BOGARDE

THE
COMPLETE
CAREER
ILLUSTRATED

ROBERT TANITCH

EBURY PRESS
LONDON

FOR ANNA QUAYLE AND DON BAKER

Also by Robert Tanitch

A PICTORIAL COMPANION TO SHAKESPEARE'S PLAYS

RALPH RICHARDSON, A TRIBUTE

OLIVIER

LEONARD ROSSITER

ASHCROFT

GIELGUD

Published by Ebury Press
Division of The National Magazine Company Limited
Colquhoun House
27–37 Broadwick Street
London W1V 1FR

First impression 1988

ISBN 0 85223 694 8

Designed by Peartree Design Associates
Filmset by Advanced Filmsetters (Glasgow) Ltd
Printed and bound in Great Britain by
Butler & Tanner Limited, Frome and London

CONTENTS

INTRODUCTION

DIRK BOGARDE is one of the screen's most distinguished actors and his performances in a wide variety of roles have won him both popular and critical acclaim. This book is a pictorial record of his career in film, theatre and television from his first appearance on the West End stage in 1940 to the present day.

In the 1950s Dirk Bogarde was the Number One Box Office Star, the Idol of the Odeons, making films aimed at family audiences. Yet because of the unrewarding roles he was so often asked to play in bad pictures, his name had little distinction as far as many of the top directors were concerned. He was thought of as a movie star rather than as an actor.

In the 1960s, working with Joseph Losey, John Schlesinger and Jack Clayton, he appeared in some of the key films of the period. His name now had distinction but he was no longer box office. Bogarde left England to live in France and work on the Continent.

By the 1970s he had become a major star of the intellectual cinema, specialising in subtle and complex roles, and European film producers could finance their films on his name. He worked with Luchino Visconti, Liliana Cavani, Alain Resnais and Rainer Werner Fassbinder.

In the 1980s, having produced four volumes of autobiography and three novels (all of which became best-sellers), he was asked if he had given up the cinema. He replied that the cinema seemed to have given him up and that he wasn't offered any interesting roles any more. His most recent work has been in television.

Bogarde has appeared in over sixty films. Initially cast as neurotics, juvenile delinquents and fugitives from justice (invariably in dirty mackintoshes), he graduated to servicemen in uniform, often equally neurotic, and romantic heroes in costume. He has played composers, painters, novelists, spies, television frontmen and any number of homosexuals.

In his time he has been a bookie, speedway champion, Borstal boy, drug-addict, penniless street-musician, army deserter, Dutch refugee, cheese salesman, medical student, newly-wed, ship's doctor, gardener (the local pelota champion), Mexican bandit, defrocked priest, barrister, research psychologist, Harley Street surgeon, manservant, intelligence officer, Oxford don, master code-breaker, British consul, schizophrenic chocolate manufacturer, and a camp villain in a cartoon-strip.

He has served in the forces, bombing Berlin, raiding an airfield in Rhodes, bailing out over the Channel, kidnapping the German C-in-C of occupied Crete, escaping from a POW camp, assisting at a court martial, and wiping out Rhoem's Brown Shirts.

He has planted bombs in London's underground, fought the Mau Mau single-handed, plunged into the maelstrom in Canada, married a Japanese girl in India, suffered from amnesia, committed suicide on at least three occasions, killed his wife's lover and made a career out of murdering rich women. He was 'the bastard' who shot P.C. Dixon. He has also been murdered, knifed on the high seas, hanged in Russia, guillotined in France, and bashed over the head with a poker in the London suburbs. . . .

Derek Niven Van den Bogaerde was born in Hampstead, London, on 28th March 1921. His father was for many years the picture editor of *The Times* and his mother before her marriage had been the actress Margaret Niven. He was educated at Allan Glen's College in Glasgow, University College School in London, and the Chelsea Polytechnic (now the Chelsea School of Art), where he took a course in commercial art and stage and film décor.

His professional career in the theatre began in 1939 when he joined the Q Theatre at Kew Bridge as stage-hand, assistant to the designer, painter of sets, boiler of glue, maker of tea, and call-boy. He graduated to stage management and later landed his first role when a member of the cast of J.B. Priestley's *When We Are Married* fell ill and he had to stand in.

His West End debut was in 1940 as Lawrence, the office boy, in a revival of J.B. Priestley's *Cornelius*, a part he had acted originally at the Q. When the play's run was curtailed by the Blitz, he joined the chorus of Herbert Farjeon's *Diversion*, a revue which braved the bombs matinées only. He then played the juvenile lead in a not particularly happy tour of Arthur Ridley's popular 1920s farce *The Ghost Train* before enlisting in the army in 1941.

Bogarde has described the Second World War as the single most significant thing in his life. ('Nothing can be as bad as war or the things I saw there.') He went into the Army Intelligence Photographic Unit, took part in the D-Day invasion, acted as unofficial war artist (the British War Museum has acquired one of his drawings), saw service in Europe and Singapore, and witnessed the horrors of Belsen. ('I realised I was looking at Dante's *Inferno*.') He was demobbed in 1946.

He resumed his stage career, coming to the notice of the critics in 1947 as the murderer in Michael Clayton Hutton's *Power Without Glory*. His success led to a seven-year contract with the J. Arthur Rank Organisation and a leading role in *Esther Waters* (1948), in which he was totally miscast. He felt his quick rise to stardom was a retrograde step: 'No actor should begin as a star. You just can't start suddenly.'

Quartet, *Once A Jolly Swagman*, *Dear Mr Prohack* and *Boys in Brown* followed in quick succession, but it wasn't until the seminal and immensely popular *The Blue Lamp* (1950) that he got his first real break. Working with Basil Dearden, a major influence in his career, he discovered for the first time that the camera could actually photograph what was going on in an actor's head. His success as the small-time criminal led to a seemingly unending supply of men-on-the-run in *Blackmailed*, *Hunted* (with six-year-old Jon Whiteley – 'one of the best films I ever made'), the IRA thriller *The Gentle Gunman* and *Desperate Moment*. He didn't get out of his dirty raincoat until the comedy *Penny Princess* (1952), when he appeared in his pyjamas. It was, he said, 'a catastrophe'.

He wore uniform for the first time in 1953, playing a war-wracked wing-commander in *Appointment in London*, directed by Philip Leacock, another important influence in his early career. This was followed by *They Who Dare*, a tribute to the Special Boat Service, whose motto, 'Who Dares Wins', took on an ironic ring when director Lewis Milestone and the cast fought a losing battle with the script. He had wanted desperately to be in *The Cruel Sea* (in the role landed by Donald Sinden) but found himself instead in *The Sea Shall Not Have Them*, a film most critics felt the sea was more than welcome to have.

The major turning point came in 1954 with *Doctor in the House* which established Bogarde as the Rank Organisation's biggest star. He always has been the first to acknowledge the enormous debt he owed to producer Betty E. Box and director Ralph Thomas for insisting that he should play the diffident medic Dr Simon Sparrow despite the serious reservations of head office as to his suitability. Such was the comedy's phenomenal success and his personal popularity in the role that he would make three sequels and still be 'doctoring' in 1963.

He then appeared in *The Sleeping Tiger*, in which he was cast as a dangerous criminal befriended by a psychiatrist and bedded by the psychiatrist's wife. The film is interesting only because it was Joseph Losey's first film in England and the start of a friendship and working partnership which would, nine years later, totally transform his career. He followed this melodrama with the comedy *For Better For Worse*, playing a young newly-wed, a role he had created at the Q Theatre back in 1948.

Five years running, from 1955 to 1960, he won the Motion Picture Academy Poll in Europe over such stars as Rock Hudson and Doris Day. He appeared first in the Mau Mau film *Simba*, which had been earmarked for Jack Hawkins, whose stolid, reliable, stiff-upper-lip, British qualities would no doubt have been more appropriate. His performance was greeted with Derek Monsey's memorable headline in the *Sunday Express*: O RARE DIRK! – HE CAN ACT. The critics would continue to express their surprise that he could act well into the Sixties.

He starred with Brigitte Bardot in *Doctor at Sea* and with Margaret Lockwood in the murder-thriller *Cast A Dark Shadow*, where to his great relief he was neither in mackintosh nor in uniform searching for salvation. He renewed his partnership with young Jon Whiteley in *The Spanish Gardener*, a watered-down version of A.J. Cronin's novel, and was then seen in the undergraduate wartime caper *Ill Met By Moonlight*, *Doctor at Large*, the Canadian western *Campbell's Kingdom*, the wartime romance *The Wind Cannot Read*, *A Tale of Two Cities*, and the courtroom drama *Libel*. All showed a keen appreciation of popular taste and relied heavily on Bogarde's attributes. ('I've got a quality, and it's called charm – and I flog it.') His fan-mail rose to four thousand letters a week.

Bogarde was perhaps at his best as Louis Dubedat, the dying scroundrel-painter in Bernard Shaw's *The Doctor's Dilemma* (1959) directed by Anthony Asquith. Jympson Harman in the *Evening News* described his death as 'one of the finest death-bed scenes since Garbo had died in *Camille*'. It would have been interesting to know what his fans had made of a film that many of them, no doubt, had come to see under the impression they were about to enjoy the latest escapades of Dr Simon Sparrow.

He had turned down *Gigi* to appear in *A Tale of Two Cities*. It would have been a far, far better thing to have made his American début as Gaston in Alan Jay Lerner and Frederick Loewe's musical than as Franz Liszt in *Song Without End* (1960), a song to forget, which emptied cinemas in a big way and effectively killed off his Hollywood career before it had begun. On the positive side, however, it had offered him the opportunity of working with George Cukor. ('I learned more from him in one film than I had learned in all the previous twenty.') He would work with Cukor again when Cukor replaced Joseph Strick on the ill-fated *Justine* (1969), a travesty of Lawrence Durrell's *The Alexandria Quartet*, in which he was cast as the disillusioned, gone-to-seed, hard-drinking Pursewarden.

He returned from Hollywood to play a Mexican bandit in love with a priest in *The Singer Not The Song*, best remembered now for its tight-fitting trousers, and a defrocked priest in love with a prostitute in *The Angel Wore Red*, which is not remembered at all.

By 1961 Bogarde had been under exclusive contract to the J. Arthur Rank Organisation for fourteen years. Fed up with playing unrewarding roles in bad movies and deeply dissatisfied with the screenplays on offer, he decided the time had come for a change of direction. He left Rank determined now to make only the films he really wanted to make.

He started with *Victim*, directed by Basil Dearden. This film, which helped to change the law on homosexuality, was a landmark in its day. His courage in risking his career by accepting the role of the homosexual barrister (a number of actors already had turned it down) was widely praised. His performance was notable for its quiet strength and moral integrity. He lost his young female fans, of course, not so much because he was playing a homosexual but rather because he was playing his own age, forty and greying.

Though *Victim* greatly enhanced his reputation he would have to wait two years and another six films for the real breakthrough. He appeared in the mutiny yarn *H.M.S. Defiant*, the POW comedy *The Password is Courage*, *We Joined the Navy* (a guest role), *The Mind Benders* (a film he thought ahead of its time), and the Judy Garland vehicle *I Could Go On Singing* ('a bit of frothy old nonsense,' he said) where his performance was appreciated for what it was: a totally self-effacing, supportive act of friendship for Garland.

He vowed in 1960 never to make another 'Doctor' film, but when *The Mind Benders* and *I Could Go On Singing* both flopped badly, he made *Doctor in Distress* to cushion himself just in case his next film flopped as well.

The Servant (1963), a Faustian black comedy, put him in the very front rank of British screen actors. Joseph Losey had wanted to make the film as early as 1956, when Bogarde would have played the seduced young lord. He now played the seducer, and when Losey fell ill with pneumonia and was in hospital for two weeks, he also took over the direction, keeping in contact by phone from the set, shot by shot. *The Servant* offered him his most substantial role to date. His subtle and witty performance was much admired and won him the best actor award from the British Film Academy.

He worked with Losey on three more occasions. The first was the anti-war *King and*

Country (1964) which, though it may not have been in the same league as Stanley Kubrick's masterpiece *Paths of Glory* (which also dealt with a court martial, one even more infamous), was still impressive and certainly vastly superior to the play on which it was based.

His casting as the camp villain in the self-indulgent, pop-art kinkiness of *Modesty Blaise* (1966) was a private joke between him and Losey; the part had been intended for Katherine Hepburn, who had turned it down at the last minute. Infinitely more satisfying was *Accident* (1967), where actor and director were perfectly attuned. ('Quite the most exciting work I have ever done on the screen.') He played an Oxford don, who was outwardly self-controlled, yet inwardly a bundle of nerves. It was, perhaps, the most difficult, the most complex, the most Pinteresque role he had played. He was quietly superb.

In between these films he was seen as an amateur spy in *Hot Enough for June* (1964) and as an intelligence officer in *The High Bright Sun* (1965) which did nothing for his reputation.

In 1965 he won the British Film Academy Award for best actor for his fine performance as the television presenter in *Darling*, one of the key films of the Sixties. He was so good that it came as a shock to learn that he had not been John Schlesinger's first choice and that he had very nearly been edited out of the film altogether.

He worked with Jack Clayton in *Our Mother's House* (1967). Charlie Hook, the long-lost father of seven children, was one of his best roles, or perhaps two of his best roles since the screenplay never did quite manage the transition from the charm of the scenes where he was larking about with the kids to the sheer brutality of the end. The film, which was badly under-estimated by the critics, was a commercial disaster; its rehabilitation is long over-due.

Bogarde was the master code-breaker in *Sebastian* (1968 – 'marshmallow disguised as food for thought', according to Liz Smith in the *New York Times*), and the Russian lawyer in *The Fixer* (1969 – 'very Hollywood, very wooden and very phoney', according to Bogarde). He also played two cameo parts for Richard Attenborough: the first was no more than a cough and a spit in *Oh! What A Lovely War* (1969); the second in *A Bridge Too Far* (1977) was more significant, his unsympathetic portrait of Sir Frederick 'Boy' Browning giving grave offence in some quarters.

Bogarde had long admired the work of Luchino Visconti. ('If he asked me to play a doorknob in one of his films, I would be a doorknob.') His first role was Bruckmann in *La Caduta Degli Dei* (1970 – *The Damned*). He might as well have been a doorknob. Two-thirds of his performance ended up on the cutting-room floor; and as for the remaining third it seemed as if the camera was always looking at his back. ('It was the best performance given by a back to a camera. . . . I was bloody good in it, though.') His second role was much more rewarding. Aschenbach, the dying composer, in Visconti's masterpiece *Morte a Venezia* (1971 – *Death in Venice*) is one of his most celebrated achievements, perhaps his greatest performance. There was hardly any dialogue; everything had to be done cerebrally. It was, he said, the hardest job he had ever had to do.

After *Death in Venice* (disconcertingly hailed by the gay community in America as 'the gay liberation movie of our time') he was offered only 'kinky teachers, neurotic priests, bent photographers and bent policemen'. He did nothing for three years and then accepted a comparatively small part in *The Serpent* to ease himself back into filming in preparation for the rigours of Liliana Cavani's *Il Portiere di Notte* (1974 – *The Night Porter*), in which he was cast as an ex-SS officer.

The Night Porter, which was based on a number of women's experiences in concentration camps, opened to a very mixed reception: acclaim, outrage, disgust and facetiousness. Some critics, such as Derek Malcolm in the *Guardian*, recognised a serious film about physical passion and guilt, while others, including Alexander Walker in the *Evening Standard*, felt the movie 'degraded the memory of the very suffering it battened on'. For Bogarde, who had made *The Night Porter* with complete sincerity, it was a horrendous experience to find the film being accused of being pornographic.

He made *Permission to Kill* (1975), an instantly forgettable political-thriller, and then worked with Alain Resnais in the stream-of-consciousness *Providence* (1976), a superb, intellectual jigsaw puzzle. (There had been talk of their making a film about the Marquis de Sade but the money never materialised.) Resnais wanted *Providence* to be like an orchestra, a quintette, in which each character was an instrument. Bogarde was the piano, sleek, arrogant, petulant and very theatrical.

He has described Rainer Werner Fassbinder, next to Visconti, as the greatest director he has ever worked with, and his performance in *Despair* (1978) as his most technically perfect, the culmination of a lifetime's work; and certainly his acting is very powerful and very impressive, even if the picture itself is flawed.

Since Bogarde became a film actor he has returned to the stage on very rare occasions. His female fans made acting in a theatre a pretty unpleasant experience, interrupting the performance with cries of 'We love you Dirk!'. The critics were often equally patronising, tending to treat him as a visiting film star rather than as an actor in his own right.

In 1950 he appeared in a more-or-less straight production of Don Boucicault's nineteenth-century melodrama, *The Shaughraun*, at the old Bedford Theatre in Camden Town. *The Times* and *Observer* found his performance as Captain Molineux, played in a deliberately quiet key, attractive, but felt it could have done with a touch more bravura.

Later the same year he played Orpheus to Mai Zetterling's Eurydice in *Point of Departure*, Jean Anouilh's contemporary version of the old legend which argued that the only way to be faithful was to be dead. Then in 1951 he was cast as the drug-addict son in the first major revival of Noël Coward's *The Vortex*, in which he was compared to Coward (who had created the role in 1924) and found wanting.

Three years later he played an Italian peasant in Ugo Betti's sentimental bubble

Summertime. John Barber, writing in the *Daily Express*, thought he was 'as graceful as a prince'. Kenneth Tynan, in the *Observer*, was less impressed: 'Dirk Bogarde, as a callow, affected youth, gives a callow, affected performance which is to pile Pelion on Ossa.'

His final appearance in the theatre was at the Oxford Playhouse in 1958 in *Jezabel*, a very early play by Jean Anouilh, which had been performed only once before in South America, and which did not look as if it would ever be performed again.

In 1961 Laurence Olivier invited him to open the newly-built Chichester Festival Theatre with 'Hamlet or some such thing'. He turned him down, knowing the critics would pull him to pieces. What Olivier should have done was invite him to play Iago to his Othello.

When Bogarde appeared in 1986 in his adaptation of Graham Greene's *May We Borrow Your Husband?*, audiences could be forgiven for thinking he was making his television début. But in fact he had appeared as early as 1947 (in the days when the BBC was still at Alexandra Palace) in Patrick Hamilton's *Rope*, Michael Clayton Hutton's *Power Without Glory* and Robert Barr's *The Case of Helvig Delbo*. He enjoyed the experience so little that he was not seen on the box again until 1965, when he did the commentary for *The Epic That Never Was*, the excellent documentary on the aborted Charles Laughton film *I, Claudius*.

In 1965 and 1966 he appeared in America in two prestigious Hallmark productions: Noël Coward's *Blithe Spirit*, with Rosemary Harris and Ruth Gordon, and James Costigan's *Little Moon Of Albion*, with Julie Harris. Three years later he made a documentary about the Basilica of St Peter's in Rome, *Upon This Rock*, playing Bonnie Prince Charlie in mufti.

Another twelve years went by before he was seen with Glenda Jackson in *The Patricia Neal Story*, playing Patricia Neal's then husband, Roald Dahl. Good though they were (Brian Winston, in the *Soho Times*, thought they both deserved an 'Emmy' nomination), the last thing the story needed was two famous actors in the leading roles.

His most recent production was William Nicholson's *The Vision* (1988), which promised a political warning and satire on satellite television and, sadly, delivered science-fiction and family melodrama.

Dirk Bogarde, an actor of versatility, intelligence, integrity, charm and technical assurance, has been at the top of his profession since the 1950s, his talents often wasted in trivia yet always clearly visible. Equally adept in extrovert and passive roles, and particularly good with ambivalent sub-texts, his acting has rightly been praised for its sensitivity, authority, candour and increasing subtlety. 'Sometimes I think I am too subtle,' he has said. 'I love the camera and it loves me. Well, not very much sometimes. But we're good friends.'

The pages which follow are a pictorial record of his long-standing affair with the camera. They are also a tribute to an actor whose performances have given enormous pleasure to fans, film buffs and critical audiences alike.

PART ONE

IDOL OF
THE ODEONS

Dirk Bogarde in 1939, aged nineteen, on
his way to audition for Tyrone Guthrie at
the Old Vic Theatre.

CORNELIUS 1940

a play by
J. B. Priestley
directed by
Henry Cass
Westminster
Theatre

Cornelius, which described the bankruptcy of an old-fashioned firm, was an allegory about the decline of capitalism. Cornelius (a role written for and created by Ralph Richardson in 1935 and played in this production by Stephen Murray) was a City aluminium broker who believed there were more important things in life than aluminium.

On the first night the air raid sirens interrupted the meeting of the creditors for a space of about a minute. *The Times* critic commented that nobody left the theatre.

Bogarde played the office boy, a role he had played a few months earlier at the Q Theatre.

Cornelius was his first West End play.

Derek Bogaerde is a sulky true-to-life office boy.   *Stage*

When Bogarde first began acting, he used his own name.

Stephen Murray, Jenny Laird, Max Adrian, Ann Wilton, Dirk Bogarde and Dorothy Hamilton in *Cornelius*.

a play by Michael
Clayton Hutton
directed by
Chloë Gibson
New Lindsay
Theatre
transferred to the
Fortune Theatre

Dirk Bogarde and
Kenneth More in
*Power Without
Glory.*

*P*ower *Without Glory* described the impact of a murder on an ordinary working-class family. Bogarde played the murderer. His performance won him a seven-year contract with the J. Arthur Rank Organisation.

Noël Coward (who had admired the play at the New Lindsay and given the management a quote to use in their publicity when it transferred to the West End) was very angry when he offered Bogarde a leading role in his play *Peace in Our Time* and found he was already signed up to play William Latch in *Esther Waters.*

Mr Bogarde is an excellent casual murderer, all egotism and nerves.

The Times

I am prepared to lay one hundred to one with anyone that this young man will make a big future for himself.

ELIZABETH FRANK *News Chronicle*

Anyone in London who really cares for vital, true and exciting acting, must see Power Without Glory *– a most moving and finely written play and on all counts an enthralling evening in the theatre.*

NOËL COWARD

I had a great success in the third act where I screamed my head off. That's why I got the notices. If you scream in the third act, you win.

DIRK BOGARDE

ESTHER WATERS   1948

directed by
Ian Dalrymple and
Peter Proud
U.S. title:
The Sin of Esther Waters

Bogarde, who had been offered the small but effective part of the priest (later played by Cyril Cusack), landed the leading role of William Latch, the gambling footman turned bookmaker who seduces the kitchen maid and then deserts her, when it was turned down by Stewart Granger. Kathleen Ryan played Esther.

All the passion and indignation had been taken out of George Moore's novel and nothing was left but the sentimental and melodramatic. A once-sensational, socio-logical Victorian document, originally banned by the libraries in the 1880s, had been turned into a tedious tear-jerker.

Bogarde, defeated by the part, the stilted language and the sluggish pace, was not alone in thinking he was totally miscast and out of his depth.

The best thing about *Esther Waters* was the reconstruction of the 1881 Derby in a lively and crowded canvas worthy of William Powell Frith.

Dirk Bogarde – a young actor who has shown considerable promise in the theatre – is likeable and feckless, but lacks entirely the loud vulgarity of William Latch.
ELIZABETH FRANK *News Chronicle*

Kathleen Ryan and Dirk Bogarde demonstrate enough ability to justify their being seen in something a little nearer their depth.
MILTON SHULMAN *Evening Standard*

Dirk Bogarde, another newcomer, justifies his quick jump to stardom.
A.E. WILSON *Star*

Dirk Bogarde,
Lelage Lewis and
Kathleen Ryan in
Esther Waters.

OPPOSITE
Dirk Bogarde and
Kathleen Ryan in
Esther Waters.

QUARTET 1948 *The Alien Corn*

directed by
Harold French

*Q*uartet, the first of the portmanteau films to be based on the short stories of Somerset Maugham, was introduced by the author himself with characteristic detachment:

'In my twenties, the critics said I was brutal, in my thirties they said I was flippant, in my forties they said I was cynical, in my fifties they said I was competent, and then in my sixties they said I was superficial.'

The shallow and uneven screenplays sentimentalised Maugham's urbane disillusionment, but the idea of seeing four films in one film caught the critics' and the public's imagination and *Quartet* scored an unexpected success, breaking records in London and New York.

The four stories were *The Facts of Life*, *The Alien Corn*, *The Kite* and *The Colonel's*

Dirk Bogarde and
Honor Blackman in
The Alien Corn.

Lady. The Alien Corn, in which Bogarde appeared, was generally considered to be the weakest of the four. He was cast as a young lord who has ambitions to be a professional pianist; when he learns he has no chance whatsoever — not in a thousand years, according to the famous French concert pianist who has been asked to pass judgement on his playing — he shoots himself.

People who knew the original story were surprised that the very kernel (the fact that he is a German Jew and doesn't *want* to be an Englishman) had been left out completely. The story was now little more than a prolonged piano recital in which the cinemagoer was invited first to watch Bogarde pretending to play competently and then to watch Françoise Rosay pretending to play brilliantly.

Honor Blackman, Irene Browne, Raymond Lovell, Françoise Rosay and Dirk Bogarde in *The Alien Corn*.

ONCE A JOLLY SWAGMAN   1948

directed by Jack Lee
U.S. title:
Maniacs on Wheels

It was somewhat ironic for somebody who had a horror of mechanics, machines and speed to find himself cast as a racing driver. Bogarde played a working-class lad, a factory hand mending light bulbs, who becomes a speedway champion and tries, unsuccessfully, to organise the riders into a militant trade union.

Once A Jolly Swagman would have been better if it had confined itself to the excitement and hysteria of the dirt-track. The documentary authenticity with which Jack Lee and cameraman Chick Fowle handled these scenes was much admired.

The actual story and the champ himself were a bore, and Bogarde, looking a right spiv, could do nothing with the part. He had one effective scene at his wedding reception when he tells the chairman of the club exactly what he feels about the conditions under which drivers have to make a living.

Dudley Jones and
Dirk Bogarde in
*Once A Jolly
Swagman.*

OPPOSITE
Dirk Bogarde in
*Once A Jolly
Swagman.*

DEAR MR PROHACK 1949

directed by
Thornton Freeland

Dirk Bogarde,
Frederick Valk,
Hermione Baddeley
and Cecil Parker
in *Dear Mr Prohack*.

*D*ear Mr Prohack, an up-dating of a minor novel by Arnold Bennett, was essentially a one-man vehicle for Cecil Parker's special talents. He played, with his usual comic pomposity and impotent fury, a senior treasury official who unexpectedly comes into a quarter of a million pounds.

The joke was in the contrast between the man's public parsimony and his private recklessness. It was a joke which went on too long, the predictable satire on Civil Service red tape disintegrating into farce and ending in an abject dream sequence.

Bogarde played Mr Prohack's son, a young man who encourages his father to put some of the money into a phoney investment trust.

a play by Michael
Clayton Hutton
directed by Michael
Clayton Hutton
Q Theatre

Dirk Bogarde and
Faith Brook in
*Sleep On My
Shoulder*.

*S*leep On My Shoulder was a trite and sentimental fantasy, in which a group of assorted characters meet in a bombed public house in Chelsea and consider what their lives are, were, and might have been. There was a great deal of pretentious dialogue.

Bogarde played an ex-RAF pilot blinded in the war who meets a girl whose sweetheart was killed in it.

The critics were not invited to see *Boys in Brown*, a film which the producers hoped would do something to awaken public interest in the cause of juvenile delinquency rather than its cure.

'How would Harrow, Eton and the rest fare,' asked Jack Warner in his role of paternalistic Governor of a Borstal Institution, 'if their intake was drawn from failures and no-goods?'

The actors, well into their twenties, and in the case of Jimmy Hanley, into his thirties, looked a wee bit old to be playing Borstal boys. Bogarde was cast as one of the no-goods, a softly-spoken Welsh loner, a sly neurotic lad and pathological liar, bent on corrupting a new inmate played by Richard Attenborough. The performance was notable for its quiet, subtle insidiousness, so quiet, in fact, as to be creepy.

I played the part with the deepest love that an actor can give a character. I didn't care a cuss if I was being unsympathetic or unromantic, or unglamorous. Take a look at my knees in this film, you'll see what I mean, but I did enjoy playing Alfie.

DIRK BOGARDE *Picturegoer*

directed by
Montgomery Tully

Jimmy Hanley, Michael Medwin, Dirk Bogarde, John Blythe and Robert Desmond in *Boys in Brown*.

OPPOSITE
Richard Attenborough and Dirk Bogarde in *Boys in Brown*.

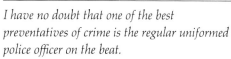

I have no doubt that one of the best preventatives of crime is the regular uniformed police officer on the beat.

MR JUSTICE FINNEMORE at the Old Bailey,
17th February, 1949.

directed by
Basil Dearden

The *Blue Lamp*, chosen as the best film of 1950 by the British Film Academy, was a major turning-point in Bogarde's career; with it he became one of Britain's most popular stars. He played a small-time criminal who, when he is caught robbing a cinema, panics and shoots a policeman.

The Blue Lamp, a semi-documentary tribute to the British bobby, belongs to those far-off days when everybody (well, practically everybody) used to think our policemen were wonderful. Scotland Yard gave the production their full co-operation and the end result was a solid public relations job which did wonders for both the Metropolitan Police's recruitment drive and the cinema's box offices.

The major weakness of the script was that it dealt in types rather than characters, the boys in blue emerging too typical and too idealised for the film's own good. The police were so delighted by Jack Warner's highly sympathetic portrait of the ideal bobby (brave, honest, humane) that they made him a freeman of all police stations. Warner would go on playing *Dixon of Dock Green* for the rest of his acting life, despite the fact that he had been shot dead halfway through the film by Bogarde.

Bogarde's young criminal, fondling the muzzle of his gun in a suggestive way, was out for cheap thrills ('I reckon a scare is good for your insides'), the latent hysteria liable at any minute to erupt in a blazing

Jack Warner and Dirk Bogarde in *The Blue Lamp.*

Peggy Evans and
Dirk Bogarde in
The Blue Lamp.

row with his girlfriend, played by Peggy
Evans, who never stopped screaming. He
represented the new breed of criminal in
post-war Britain — the amateur who brings
the profession into disrespect — and
perhaps the most endearing sight was the
tic-tac men at the White City Stadium
actually helping the police to track him
down in the milling crowds at the
greyhound race.

Bogarde has said that *The Blue Lamp* was
the first time he came near to giving a
cinema performace in any kind of depth and
described all that had gone before as
cardboard and one-dimensional. The film
would lead to a seemingly never-ending
supply of criminals-on-the-run in dirty
mackintoshes.

*Everyone used to tell me not to act in front of a
camera. Don't move a muscle of your face,
make no big gestures, keep your voice low, and,
above all, remember that you are not in a
theatre. And I believed them. Poor old Bogarde!
I went up into the world of the stars like a
damp rocket, and fell silently to earth in no
flurry of sparks. Of course you have to* act *in
front of a camera. It's quite different acting
from the stage, but you simply* must *act. At
least,* I *must. When* The Blue Lamp *started
Basil said to me: 'Act as if you were on the
stage. I'll stop you if you go too far.' And so I
did.*   DIRK BOGARDE *Picturegoer*

Dirk Bogarde in his first 'heavy' role shows that he can really act and produces a lifelike study of the modern guy who is not, after all, so smart. *Focus*

Mr Dirk Bogarde, as a representative of the new type of criminal, the reckless youth with a kink in his mind, gives an admirable performance. *The Times*

Dirk Bogarde and Patrick Doonan as hold-up gangsters touch at times the nerve of reality. William Whitebait *New Statesman and Nation*

Dirk Bogarde, the boy gangster, gets star-billing but it is the Harrow Road which is the real villain. Paul Holt *Daily Herald*

Dirk Bogarde and Peggy Evans in *The Blue Lamp.*

SO LONG AT THE FAIR   1950

directed by
Terence Fisher and
Anthony
Darnborough

Jean Simmons and
Dirk Bogarde in
So Long At The Fair.

So Long At The Fair was a variation on that classic mystery story of the visitor who vanishes at the time of the Great Exhibition, Paris, 1889. A girl loses not only her brother in the middle of the night but his hotel bedroom as well. It was generally agreed that to lose a brother might be regarded as a misfortune, but to lose a brother *and* his hotel bedroom looked like carelessness.

What had happened was that the brother had been taken ill in the night and when the doctor diagnosed that he had the plague, the authorities thought it best to hush it up, fearing tourists would boycott Paris; and Paris, expecting twenty million visitors, could not afford for the Great Exhibition to be a flop.

Jean Simmons as the *pauvre petite* whom nobody believes was charming and very pretty. She might have been more frightened if they had stuck to the original story and she had lost her mother. There were times when it seemed as if she had lost no more than her purse or pet dog.

Bogarde had the unrewarding role of the English painter who turns amateur sleuth to help her.

It was left to Cathleen Nesbitt, highly effective as the sinister hotel-proprietor, to provide the melodramatic *frissons* the story demanded.

The art decoration of Cedric Dawe was excellent.

The Woman In Question was a straightforward whodunnit handled in an original way. The police, carrying out their investigations into the murder of a seaside fortune-teller, question five people and come up with five different impressions of her character.

The film didn't really come off. The idea was always better than the script, which dealt in stereotypes. Jean Kent, one of the most popular sex symbols of British films in the 1940s, divided the critics, many thinking she was not really up to the subtle changes of character the role needed. She was certainly more convincing as the vulgar tart than as the refined lady.

Bogarde was cast as one of the suspects, a small-time music-hall pianist who wanted the woman to take part in his mind-reading act. It wasn't much of a part, though he had one effective scene when he turns down her advances and she loses her temper.

directed by
Anthony Asquith

Susan Shaw,
Dirk Bogarde and
Jean Kent in *The Woman in Question.*

POINT OF DEPARTURE   1950

a play by
Jean Anouilh
directed by
Peter Ashmore
Lyric Theatre,
Hammersmith
transferred to the
Duke of York's
Theatre

ORPHEUS: *I don't want to die. I hate death.*
MON. HENRI: *You're unfair. Why should you
hate death? She is beautiful. She
alone can create the perfect
setting for love.*

Point of Departure, Anouilh's ironic re-working of the Orpheus and Eurydice myth, is set in the refreshment room of a modern French provincial station and a bedroom in a sordid Marseilles hotel.

Orpheus (Dirk Bogarde) is a penniless street-musician and Eurydice (Mai Zetterling) is an actress in a fifth-rate touring-company. They fall in love, but she fails to live up to his idealised expectations, having neither the purity nor the strength he sees in her. The happiness they both seek can be found only in death.

Orpheus's raptures and regrets present the actor with almost as many difficulties as opportunities; but Mr Dirk Bogarde never allows this to be seen, and plays an awkward part with assurance and complete success.   PETER FLEMING *Spectator*

Miss Zetterling reduces all her rhythms to a monotonous Swedish gush; while Mr Dick Bogarde reduces his to a series of rough and over-intense emotional outbursts. A great deal of acting goes on and some of it is very good, as the acting of acting, but it is for the most part strictly irrelevant to the play. They shout and weep, they laugh and groan. But they miss almost entirely the subtlety and variety of their speeches, and that loss is fatal.

T.C. WORSLEY *New Statesman and Nation*

Mai Zetterling and
Dirk Bogarde in
Point of Departure.

OPPOSITE
Stephen Murray and
Dirk Bogarde in
Point of Departure.

BLACKMAILED 1951

directed by
Marc Allegret

Dirk Bogarde and
Harold Huth in
Blackmailed.

BELOW
Dirk Bogarde and
Fay Compton in
Blackmailed.

A blackmailer (James Robertson Justice) is accidentally killed by a kind-hearted almoner (Fay Compton). Bogarde played one of his victims, an army deserter, living with a juvenile delinquent who has escaped from a reform school. In attempting to make his getaway down a fire-escape, he loses his grip and falls to his death.

The film, described by C.A. Lejeune in the *Observer* as one of Britain's worst, was dismissed by the critics as trite, slipshod, slow-moving and resolutely mediocre.

... and sympathy goes out to poor Mr Bogarde who once again finds himself enveloped in a dirty mackintosh, the eternal deserter, eternally on the run.

The Times

Hunted, an unpretentious, efficient, low-budget thriller, was about two unwilling companions, both fugitives — a man-on-the-run who had murdered his wife's lover and a little boy running away from his brutal foster parents. It was the developing relationship between them which gave the film its special resonance and appeal, the boy finding an affection he had never known before.

Six-year-old Jon Whiteley, with his wistful, craggy, grave face, his shock of fair hair, and his Scottish accent, was incredibly natural, his touching performance obviously owing a great deal to the tact and sensitivity of the director and actor. He hardly spoke, Charles Crichton wisely letting the camera do his acting for him.

A lesser actor than Bogarde would have been annihilated; instead he gave one of his finest performances, the change of heart from open antagonism to muted tenderness perfectly gauged and never mawkish.

There were two scenes in particular — the first when irritated by the boy's silent reproach he blows his top and the second when he grudgingly buys the boy a meal in a café — where the rapport between actor and child was quite extraordinary.

Only the end didn't work. It wasn't so much that his self-sacrifice was far too sentimental but that the situation which made the self-sacrifice necessary was so artificially contrived as to have a tacked-on feeling, as if nobody had been quite certain how to finish the film.

The location work, in London, the Potteries, the Yorkshire Moors and a remote Scottish fishing village, was excellent.

BELOW
Kay Walsh, Jon Whiteley and Dirk Bogarde in *Hunted.*

directed by
Charles Crichton
U.S. title: *The Stranger in Between*

ABOVE AND RIGHT
Dirk Bogarde and
Jon Whiteley in
Hunted.

The attachment between the hunted man
and the unwanted child is presented with a
reticence and sincerity which raises a
routine escape story to something above
the level of mere competence.

WILLIAM WHITEBAIT *Time and Tide*

Dirk Bogarde in
Hunted.

The British cinema is particularly addicted
to the chase *motif* and Mr Dirk Bogarde is
the champion of those who get chased. If
there was an Olympic cross-town-and-
country event for film actors, Mr Bogarde
would start as favourite by virtue of the
fantastic amount of practice he has had.

The Times

The discipline involved in playing with
and to a child seems to have found new
reserves of strength in Dirk Bogarde's
acting.   C.A. Lejeune *Observer*

*P*enny Princess was a farce about a poor New York shop-girl inheriting a tiny bankrupt European principality and putting it on a commercial footing by exporting alcoholic cheese made from sheep's milk and schnapps.

Yolande Donlan, who had scored a big success on the London stage as the dumb blonde in *Born Yesterday*, backed the film with her own money and played the leading role with vivacity; but the script, the stuff of musical comedy without the music, was just not funny enough.

The Rank Organisation had thought of casting an American actor like William Holden to act opposite her. They ended up, largely due to his persistence, with Bogarde, desperate to do comedy. He wasn't very good.

Dirk Bogarde, a serious young actor, has a certain amount of trouble trying to be romantically funny in pyjamas.

FRED MAJDALANY *Daily Mail*

directed by
Val Guest

Laurence Naismith and Dirk Bogarde in *Penny Princess.*

THE VORTEX   1952

a play by
Noël Coward
directed by
Michael MacOwan
Lyric Theatre,
Hammersmith

*T*he Vortex, a brilliant *succès de scandale* in 1924, bringing Noël Coward overnight fame, was hardly likely to shock audiences nearly thirty years later. The once-fashionably unwholesome mix of cocktails, cocaine and post-war hysteria had become a collector's item.

Bogarde was cast in the Coward role of the neurotic, piano-strumming, drug-taking son of the house whose mother is having an affair with a man no older than himself. He was inevitably compared to Coward and found wanting, especially in the Hamlet-Gertrude-like theatrics of the third act. The play belonged to Isabel Jeans, an elegant and witty high-comedy actress, who was most moving in the final scene.

Dirk Bogarde,
Sylvia Coleridge,
Isabel Jeans,
Anthony Forwood,
Janet Butler,
Peter Jones,
Adrianne Allen and
Robert Andrews in
The Vortex.

Dirk Bogarde has not enough inner tension for the dope-ridden son.

HAROLD HOBSON *Sunday Times*

Dirk Bogarde uses the vintage piece to prove himself one of the most talented and brilliant of young actors.

R.M. *Daily Graphic*

Dirk Bogarde has to meet the challenge of the original performance in which Coward the author had tailored it for himself. Mr Bogarde is very good up to a point, but misses the Mongolian inexpressiveness of Coward's face and the hollow ironic mockery of Coward's voice.

BEVERLEY BAXTER *Evening Standard*

Dirk Bogarde's rendering of the young man whose nerves are on edge was never more than adequate, when nothing less than a *tour de force* was demanded.

REGINALD P.M. GIBBS *Daily Telegraph*

Isabel Jeans and Dirk Bogarde in *The Vortex*.

THE GENTLE GUNMAN   1952

directed by
Basil Dearden

Dirk Bogarde,
Joseph Tomelty and
John Mills in
The Gentle Gunman.

The situation in England is always serious, never hopeful. The situation in Ireland is always hopeless, never serious.

ROGER MacDOUGALL

The *Gentle Gunman*, a mixture of thriller and classroom debate, was set in 1941, first in London where the British were being bombed by both the Germans and the IRA, and then in Ireland where the IRA were shooting themselves.

John Mills was the gentle gunman, an ex-terrorist, converted to pacifism and branded a traitor by his former mates. Bogarde had the less interesting role of his brother; wearing the inevitable dirty mac and furrowed brow, he spent his time planting bombs in Holborn underground station and lugging a wounded James Kenney all over the rugged-boulder countryside, an exercise to which neither actor brought any conviction.

The highly simplistic debate – 'England

is not at war with Ireland, but Ireland is at war with England' – was conducted by Gilbert Harding, who had made a career out of being the worst-tempered man in Britain in *What's My Line?*, and Joseph Tomelty. Harding played his irascible self; Tomelty did the acting.

The message of the original Roger MacDougall play is that violence corrupts. The message of the box office, however, is that violence puts bums on seats. Easily the best sequence, finely photographed and finely edited, was the one in which the IRA attempted to stop a police van; the ensuing panic as parents attempted to sweep their children off the street had a cinematic grittiness and excitement the rest of the film's staginess badly needed.

The Gentle Gunman ended with Mills and Bogarde striding off into the distance, though where they were going and why was not at all clear; they looked for all the world like a grown-up version of that famous pre-war advert for Start-Rite shoes.

Dirk Bogarde and
John Mills in
The Gentle Gunman.

APPOINTMENT IN LONDON   1953

directed by
Philip Leacock

Dinah Sheridan and
Dirk Bogarde in
*Appointment in
London*.

The 1950s were a time when the British film industry never stopped re-fighting the Second World War. *Appointment in London*, a tribute to Bomber Command, made with the co-operation of the Air Ministry, offered no new perspective on the war and the characters were drawn strictly from stiff-upper-lip stock.

Bogarde's role of the wing commander who has flown too long — eighty-seven sorties and driving himself on to his ninetieth raid because he knows he is afraid — came of a long line of officers who had cracked under the strain, going right back to Stanhope in R.C. Sherriff's *Journey's End* (which he had played in 1938 as an amateur actor), and right up to Gregory Peck and *Twelve O'Clock High*.

The wing commander, having been grounded, disobeys orders and takes an aeroplane up on a vital bombing-raid over Germany which afforded a spectacular climax, using actual newsreels taken at the time.

The critics were delighted to find Bogarde in uniform, his hair cut, clean-shaven, and not a dirty mac in sight.

There was nothing wrong with the spiv but we were seeing him a little too often.
ROY NASH *Star*

Dirk Bogarde, happily escaped from the world of spivs and crooks, steps into the front rank of English screen actors.
CAMPBELL DIXON *Daily Telegraph*

This, if I may quite seriously put it, is Mr Bogarde's finest hour, whether discreetly conveying the inward and spiritual grace of a born leader or the outward signs of a young lover, he never slops over into implausibility.
ROBERT OTTAWAY *Sunday Graphic*

Desperate Moment was a romantic thriller with Bogarde yet again on the run, this time in Germany. He played an ex-member of the Dutch resistance, who escapes from prison to clear his name of a murder he had confessed to but not committed.

Much of the film was shot on location in the ruins of Berlin.

Dirk Bogarde, who improves with each picture, gives a first-rate performance as the innocent victim.

RON WHITELEY *Daily Mirror*

If only all the other actors in the British film industry would stop chasing Dirk Bogarde from credit titles to final fade-out in every picture he is called on to make, maybe the poor fellow could develop into a really good artist with romantic appeal possibilities as yet unrevealed.

E. HODGSON *News of the World*

directed by
Compton Bennett

Mai Zetterling and
Dirk Bogarde in
Desperate Moment.

THEY WHO DARE 1954

**directed by
Lewis Milestone**

They Who Dare was about a wartime raid on Rhodes's two airfields by members of the SBS (Special Boat Service), a commando-like sabotage group, commanded by an incompetent and very highly-strung lieutenant, played by Bogarde, clambering over rocks, carrying the world on his conscience. You knew from the start that he was going to make a hash of everything when he was seen, sporting a silk scarf, discussing the secret mission in a night-club full of eavesdropping *femmes fatales*. Out of a crew of six Brits and four Greeks, only two Brits survived.

'I hate you. I hate you for not giving up. You don't know when you're licked!'

Dirk Bogarde and
Denholm Elliott in
They Who Dare.

screamed Denholm Elliott, in his role of intellectual sergeant who was given to quoting W.H. Auden and Rupert Brooke in an emergency. 'The whole thing's a shambles,' admitted Bogarde, probably referring to the lack of a script, the original screenplay having been chucked away by Lewis Milestone as he stepped off the plane. The hysterical antagonism of the two men came out of absolutely nothing and was constantly having to be revved up with lines like *Don't cloak cheap gestures with noble motives* and *Now look what you've gone and done. You've spoiled everything.*

There was some excitement on the airfield, but for the most part the excitement was so artificially contrived as to make any involvement impossible. The end was a dreadful cheat, too, with the actors one minute floundering in the water liable to be shot and the very next rescued, on board a ship, and no indication as to how it had been achieved. So often were climaxes delivered without any preparation that audiences inevitably felt they were not watching the whole film.

The disappointment with *They Who Dare* (known in the business as *How Dare They*) was increased by the knowledge that it was directed by the man who had directed *All Quiet on the Western Front*, one of the great war movies of all time. Only one panoramic tracking shot of the search party advancing on the camera had the unmistakable Milestone signature.

Dirk Bogarde spends most of his time apologising to his crew for the mistakes he makes. Nobody apologises for the script.
HARRIS DEANS *Sunday Dispatch*

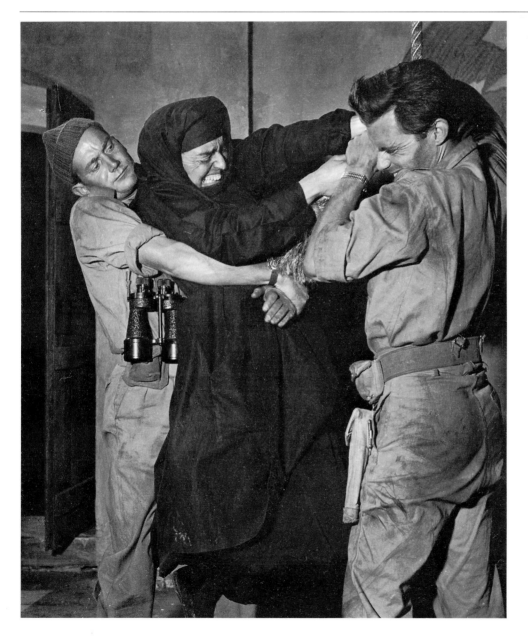

Denholm Elliott,
Eileen Way and
Dirk Bogarde in
They Who Dare.

Further, while the script is to blame for the lines the leader Lieutenant Graham has to say, Mr Dirk Bogarde cannot escape responsibility for making bad worse.

The Times

Dirk Bogarde, Denholm Elliott and Akim Tamiroff who play the leads were never better.

PETER BURNUP *News of the World*

DOCTOR IN THE HOUSE   1954

directed by
Ralph Thomas

Doctor in the House, a jolly if not exactly original anthology of medical-student gags, adapted from Richard Gordon's novel, was the biggest hit of the year, the start of a never-ending series on film and television.

Kenneth More, straight from his success in *Genevieve*, was very amusing as the perpetually-failing student, and he would most certainly have walked off with the film, with his boisterous, immensely likeable, natty-waistcoated performance, if it had not been for James Robertson Justice walking off with the film. Justice played the eminent surgeon, Sir Lancelot Spratt, the red-bearded terror of St Swithins, with enormous gusto, bestriding the corridors, wards and operating theatres while staff and students walked under his huge legs to peep about and find themselves dishonourable graves. The viva voce he shared with More was one of the funniest scenes in the film.

It said a great deal for Bogarde, in the potentially unrewarding role of Simon Sparrow, foil and romantic lead, that he was not overwhelmed by these two flamboyant actors. The naïvety and diffidence was acted with great charm. There was a delightful moment when he put his stethoscope to his ears for the first time and admitted, with doe-eyed wonderment, that he could hear the sea. The sentimental scene in which, on his first maternity case, he delivers a baby without the assistance of a midwife, was a bit of genuine feeling amid all the horse-play, touchingly played by him and Maureen Pryor.

Doctor in the House was a major turning-point in Bogarde's career. He became Rank's biggest star.

Donald Sinden,
Kenneth More,
Dirk Bogarde and
Donald Houston in
Doctor in the House.

Clockwise round the piano:
Dirk Bogarde,
Noel Purcell,
Suzanne Cloutier,
Kenneth More,
Donald Houston and
Donald Sinden in
Doctor in the House.

Mr Bogarde, wearing a youthfully lost look, displays a gift for comedy I don't remember seeing before.

Roy Nash *Star*

Mr Bogarde shines in a part unlike those to which he is normally condemned.

The Times

How nice to see him released from playing neurotic cosh boys of all ages.

Peter Wilshire *Sunday Chronicle*

And Dirk Bogarde as the central figure suddenly shows a gift for comedy unsuspected in the player of heroic desperadoes we have so often met.

Dilys Powell *Sunday Times*

It is perhaps the final achievement of this extravaganza that it endears you to the health service.

Fred Majdalany *Daily Mail*

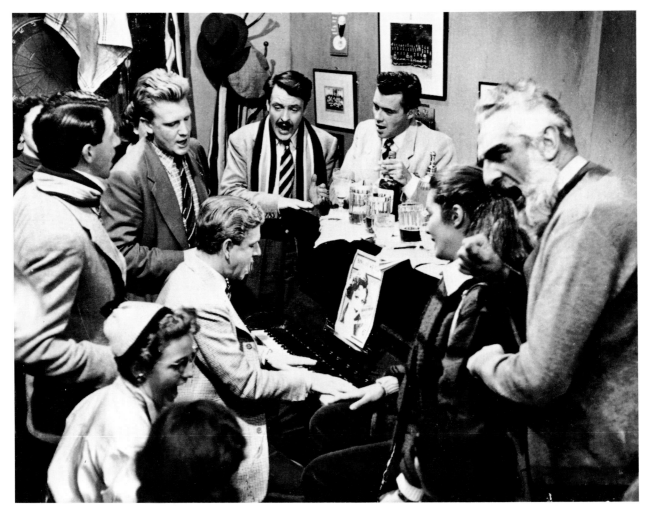

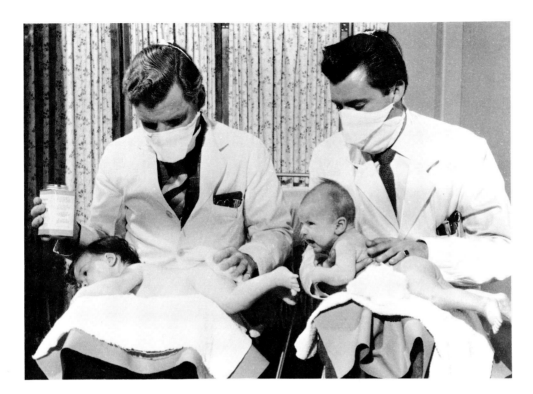

Kenneth More and
Dirk Bogarde in
Doctor in the House.

BELOW
Dirk Bogarde,
Maureen Pryor and
Amy Veness in
Doctor in the House.

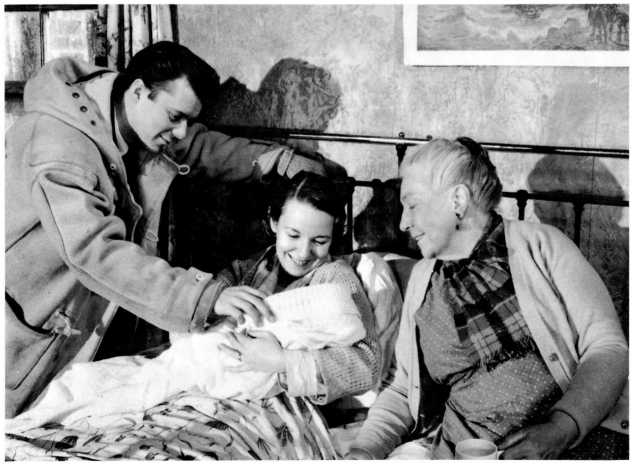

THE SLEEPING TIGER   1954

directed by
Joseph Losey

Dirk Bogarde and
Alexis Smith in
The Sleeping Tiger.

Joseph Losey, blacklisted by Hollywood (a victim of Senator McCarthy and his Committee of Un-American Activities), came to England and was offered *The Sleeping Tiger*, which he worked on under the pseudonym of Victor Hanbury.

In order to persuade Bogarde to do the film he showed him two of his own: a remake of *M* and *The Prowler*. It was the beginning of a friendship and working relationship which would, nine years later, transform Bogarde's career.

Neither of them had any illusions about the script, which Losey described as 'a lousy cheap story... a sort of bedtime reading for senile stags'. But he needed the work and was grateful for it; and grateful to Bogarde, too, acknowledging that his 'career, and even the existence of a career' had been made possible by Bogarde's acceptance.

The Sleeping Tiger 'explored the darker forces of every human personality where lurks a sleeping tiger'. Bogarde was cast in his usual role of neurotic criminal. This time he was befriended by a very busy psychiatrist who, in an unlikely six-month experiment, took him into his home, in the belief that he could cure him with kindness and the occasional chat. When the psychiatrist discovered his patient had been having it off with his wife, he pretended to shoot him dead. Most people thought the psychiatrist was in need of a psychiatrist.

The film may have been set in England; but its soul remained firmly in Hollywood, with everybody (and especially Malcolm Arnold's score) behaving as if they were in a 1940s Joan Crawford movie. The denouement, in which Alexis Smith as the hysterical wife drives to her death, crashing through a hoarding carrying an Esso tiger advertisement, was a fitting climax to all the nonsense that had gone before.

Dirk Bogarde in
The Sleeping Tiger.

We thought the script itself was frightful and it embarrassed us incredibly to do it.
DIRK BOGARDE

But good writing makes for good acting, and Mr Bogarde's young criminal must be regarded as one of the finest film performances of the year.
BEVERLEY BAXTER *Evening Standard*

Bogarde gives a sterling if typical performance.
ELIZABETH FRANK *News Chronicle*

Dirk Bogarde plays his usual part of attractive, reformable not quite grown-up delinquency.
Manchester Guardian

With this film, in fact, Bogarde graduates from the class of feather-weight heroes. With *Doctor in the House* recently to his credit, he has become the most versatile middle-weight we have.
ROBERT OTTAWAY *Sunday Graphic*

FOR BETTER FOR WORSE 1954

directed by
J. Lee-Thompson

*F*or Better For Worse, based on a popular West End stage success, was a cosy, very English comedy about the trials of two charming newly-weds living in a one-room flat. The play was written by the British film censor, A.T.L. Watkins, under the pseudonym Arthur Watkyn.

Roy Nash, in the *Evening Standard*, idly wondered what the American censor would say about Bogarde and Susan Stephen being in bed together (even though they were doing nothing). These were the days when actors in bedroom scenes were still expected to have one foot on the floor.

The British censor took offence at only one line, 'I shall laugh my bleeding head off,' and the 'bleeding' was changed to 'flipping'.

Susan Stephen and
Dirk Bogarde in
For Better For Worse.

FAR RIGHT
Dirk Bogarde in
For Better For Worse.

Dirk Bogarde is fast becoming one of our most accomplished light comedians.
HAROLD CONWAY *Daily Sketch*

Bogarde, who strikes me as one of the three best young actors in British film and Susan Stephen, act well. Their scenes together are full of tender charm.
ROY NASH *Evening Standard*

Bogarde (though nobody seemed to be aware of it) had created his role at the Q Theatre, Kew Bridge, in the play's try-out in 1948, where it was well received by *The Times*:

What is charming in the farcical proceedings is the perfect gravity with which the young couple conduct themselves. Miss Margaret Barton and Mr Dirk Bogarde are young enough and appealing enough to make an elderly sentimentalist regard them with indulgence, though one suspects that the cold hard eye of youth may see in the characters they represent so engagingly a travesty of a very serious generation.
The Times

THE SEA SHALL NOT HAVE THEM   1954

directed by
Lewis Gilbert

Dirk Bogarde in
*The Sea Shall Not
Have Them.*

When British actresses heard that the studios were going to make yet another war film, they complained bitterly that they were not being given their fair share of screen time; they were fractionally less bitter when they heard that the actors who had spent three weeks in cold sea water had all developed boils.

The Sea Shall Not Have Them was a belated tribute to the Air Sea Rescue Services. Four airmen sat in a dinghy after bailing out over the Channel. There wasn't much for the actors to do except wait to be rescued. Michael Redgrave clutched a briefcase said to be full of secret plans for a new German weapon. Bogarde played a flight sergeant worrying about his shop in London and a court martial for fiddling petrol.

While the war was actually on this rough approximation to reality served admirably, but, now that it is some distance away, the inadequacies of the formulae, its failure imaginatively to illumine physical ordeal and spiritual experiences, becomes more obvious.   *The Times*

Actors cannot act without material, and an almost unlimited session in a rubber dinghy, as presented in this picture, is just not actable.

WILLIAM DOUGLAS HOME *Evening Standard*

My main quarrel with the picture is the misuse – or non-use – of Michael Redgrave's and Dirk Bogarde's talents. Redgrave may be a VIP in the script but he's a nonentity in the dinghy. And Bogarde, who can thrill or amuse at will, has to spend most of the time grizzling.

HAROLD CONWAY *Daily Sketch*

SIMBA 1955

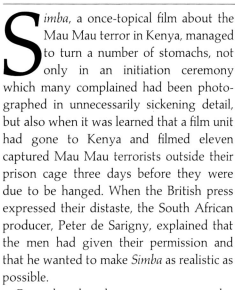

*S*imba, a once-topical film about the Mau Mau terror in Kenya, managed to turn a number of stomachs, not only in an initiation ceremony which many complained had been photographed in unnecessarily sickening detail, but also when it was learned that a film unit had gone to Kenya and filmed eleven captured Mau Mau terrorists outside their prison cage three days before they were due to be hanged. When the British press expressed their distaste, the South African producer, Peter de Sarigny, explained that the men had given their permission and that he wanted to make *Simba* as realistic as possible.

Bogarde played a young man who arrives in Kenya to find his brother has been murdered and determines to exact his revenge. He is himself very nearly murdered but saved in the nick of time, U.S. cavalry-fashion, by the very black doctor he had suspected of being the terrorist leader.

Stepping off the plane at the beginning of the film, in his felt hat, he looked for a moment his usual screen-criminal self. His performance was in his familiar pent-up, edgy manner and his exchanges with Earl Cameron (the black doctor) were very theatrical.

There was a love scene with Virginia McKenna in a very English field, which was described by some critics as one of the most convincing love scenes ever filmed; it was in fact far from being convincing and sounded like a parody of women's magazine fiction as acted by Noël Coward.

The actors remained in England. One of the disadvantages of this was that in a key scene when a lion had to attack Simba (the

directed by
Brian Desmond
Hurst

Donald Sinden and
Dirk Bogarde in
Simba.

59

Dirk Bogarde and Virginia McKenna in *Simba*.

name of a fictional Mau Mau leader) the lion and the actor, Orlando Martins, were so obviously in two separate films as to make the scene ridiculous. Nor were matters helped by the lion, a very cuddly-looking lion, who quite clearly had never acted in his life and gave a quite appalling performance.

Simba benefited enormously from the tactful understatement Basil Sydney and Marie Ney brought to their scenes as the elderly couple everybody knows will be murdered before they can retire to England.

The trouble is not that this film shocks by realism, but that nine-tenths of it is on a fictional level that makes realism distasteful.

WILLIAM WHITEBAIT
New Statesman and Nation

But one is always aware of the bland assumption that the British belong in Kenya, that they have a God-given right to usurp the best grazing lands, and that their treatment of the natives is for their ultimate good. The racial antagonism, which is probably real enough, is shown, but the economic motivations are not. Colonel Blimp is not actually in the movie but his shadow hovers over it.

Saturday Review

The acting is magnificent. Dirk Bogarde goes from strength to strength.

WILLIAM DOUGLAS HOME *Evening Standard*

Bogarde has one of those taut, truculent, anti-pathetic character parts which he plays with beautiful precision. And goes on playing, time after time. Yet, given the opportunity, he can play the lover and he can play intelligent, sensitive parts. Among British stars he is that rare animal, a very fine actor. But you can kill the best actor – or the topmost star – with too many stereotyped and unsympathetic parts. The problem is – can Bogarde survive?

DEREK MONSEY *Sunday Express*

DOCTOR AT SEA 1955

**directed by
Ralph Thomas**

It was not surprising that Betty E. Box and Ralph Thomas should want to cash in on the phenomenal success of *Doctor in the House*, the most profitable British film comedy ever made. The sequel, however, obviously aimed at a different, down-market audience, was very disappointing. The script was broader, cruder, more farcical, and far less funny than the original. There were predictable jokes about being sea-sick, extracting teeth and getting drunk. The molar provided the most fun. The rest was pretty dire. The temptation to abandon ship was enormous. The funniest thing really was being expected to take seriously Dr Simon Sparrow's operation on the quartermaster's appendix with the assistance of the only two female passengers.

The film lacked spontaneity. It also lacked Kenneth More. It did have James Robertson Justice. In fact the biggest surprise was to find that Sir Lancelot Spratt was the ship's captain masquerading under the name of Hogg. The second surprise was that Sparrow didn't seem to notice; he

Dirk Bogarde and
Brigitte Bardot in
Doctor at Sea.

didn't even raise an eyebrow. James Robertson Justice made no effort to differentiate between the two men: he bawled everybody out and generally behaved as if he were a rogue elephant on heat.

Bogarde acted the silly anything-for-a-laugh jokes and incidents with commendable restraint, keeping his sea-legs while all around him were going wildly overboard. He was his normal shy, amiable, unassertive, Sparrow self. The producers provided him with a new girlfriend – the nineteen-year-old Brigitte Bardot, making her wide-eyed debut in a British film.

Doctor at Sea was a huge success and Bogarde was voted the most popular actor in Great Britain in 1955.

Dirk Bogarde takes to the role of the doctor as if he had been born with a stethoscope in his mouth.

MILTON SHULMAN *Sunday Express*

Dirk Bogarde, again the young doctor, is developing a polished technique.

DILYS POWELL *Sunday Times*

Maurice Denham, Dirk Bogarde and George Coulouris in *Doctor at Sea.*

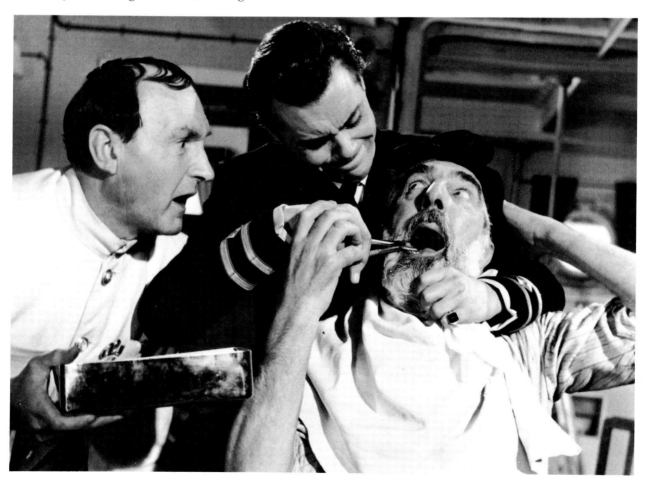

CAST A DARK SHADOW 1955

directed by
Lewis Gilbert

Phillip Stainton,
Dirk Bogarde and
Margaret Lockwood
in *Cast A Dark
Shadow*.

Cast A Dark Shadow was based on a play and it showed, a stagey unreality informing every line. There was in fact more script than film.

Bogarde was cast as an estate agent's clerk: a smooth charmer who marries and murders older women for their money. The role was a not-too-distant relation of Danny in Emlyn Williams's *Night Must Fall*.

It was clear from the close-ups of Bogarde's face and the framing of one or two shots that the cameraman, Jack Asher, could have provided an atmospheric baroque thriller; but he was working with a director who eschewed the visual thrills a murdered woman's locked bedroom or a conversation at a cliff's edge might provide. The story badly needed the Hitchcock touch.

Margaret Lockwood's performance as his victim-to-be, a cockney ex-barmaid, was generally thought to be the best thing she had ever done, the brassy vulgarity of her acting taking everybody by surprise; but the real surprise was that the big scene in

Dirk Bogarde in
Cast A Dark Shadow.

the film was not between her and Bogarde but between Bogarde and Kay Walsh, hamming away in a hysterical vacuum. Her own scene, which followed on immediately, petered out before it had even begun, the director strangely uninterested in the melodramatic possibilities of a woman all alone in an empty house with a homicidal maniac.

There could be only one reason why the barmaid should want to shack up with the estate agent and that must be because he was good in bed. 'Quite a little jockey,' she observes at one point. The 'jockey' was missing in Bogarde's performance, which could have done with a bit more glib charm. He preferred to concentrate on the transparent nastiness and understandable paranoia of a fortune-hunter who had killed the golden goose (also his surrogate mother) and is unable to satisfy the voracious sexual appetite of his new wife. 'I didn't marry you for companionship,' she tells him. As always, Bogarde was very good at conveying the essential weakling underneath the ruthless, cold-blooded exterior.

Dirk Bogarde, leaving his doctor at sea, resumes murdering with his sinister polish unimpaired.

HAROLD CONWAY *Daily Sketch*

There is a brilliantly disgusting performance from Dirk Bogarde, allowed not only to play a murderer without a raincoat for once, but to act as well.

DEREK MONSEY *Sunday Express*

There is admirable credibility in Dirk Bogarde's scapegrace young murderer of moneyed women.

PAUL DEHN *News Chronicle*

It is very well acted by Mr Bogarde as snide a young bluebeard as ever murdered ageing wife for sordid gain.

MAURICE WILLSHIRE *Daily Mail*

For myself, I only claim one thing. I am an actor – it's taken me years, but I think I am an actor now. I act in films and I'm glad to take the money, but I'm not a film star *and never have been.*

DIRK BOGARDE quoted by
GERALD BOWMAN *Evening News*

THE SPANISH GARDENER   1956

directed by
Philip Leacock

The Spanish Gardener was about an embittered and stuffed-shirted British diplomat (Michael Hordern) who becomes so jealous of his small son's affection for the gardener that he has the man unjustly prosecuted for pilfering.

Bogarde, certainly no Spaniard either in speech or gesture, and surprisingly well spoken and articulate, acted with a gentleness which was immensely appealing. It was a skilful, quiet, dignified performance matching the film's own restraint.

The relationship with the boy (Jon Whiteley) was sensitively handled; so sensitively handled that it was easy to miss what was really going on. In the original A.J. Cronin story, the possessive father, with his selfish and demanding love, was the leading character and he was in love with the gardener as well. This was something the Rank Organisation preferred to ignore, though in one confrontation in which he emerged the easy victor ('I don't know what evil there is in your mind, but I pity your son') Bogarde was able to hint that he at least was aware of a sub-text.

The career of the slim and handsome Dirk Bogarde takes a large stride forward this week with his latest film. . . . Now he gets a part worthy of his talents.

ANTHONY CARTHEW *Daily Herald*

But it is Dirk Bogarde, with his lazy friendliness and doe-eyed charm as the Spanish gardener who befriends the lonely boy who dominates the picture.

ELIZABETH FRANK *News Chronicle*

Jon Whiteley and
Dirk Bogarde in
The Spanish Gardener.

Ill Met By Moonlight was based on Patrick Leigh Fermor's account of a wartime escapade in 1941, when he was involved in abducting General Karl Kreipe (Marius Goring), the Divisional Commander of occupied Crete, from under the eyes of the Germans.

The film, which never matched the cheeky bravado of the original story, was slackly directed, murkily photographed (ill-lit by moonlight) and enormously un-exciting, having about as much suspense as a Sunday afternoon walk in picturesque scenery. Here was an adventure story without any adventure.

The incredibly noisy Cretan partisans spoke Greek (without subtitles, to the annoyance of some critics) and generally behaved as if they were in a third-rate opera touring company, the soundtrack bursting absurdly into patriotic singing every time they appeared. The Germans were usually to be seen studying a map. It would have made better dramatic sense if they had been seen scouring the countryside.

Bogarde, sporting a bandit moustache and dressed in Greek national costume, began on a camp-flirtatious note, striking a mock-Byronic pose. Later, in uniform, he acted with studied casualness, in keeping, no doubt, with Leigh Fermor's own laconic line in languid, unaffected self-deprecation, but for such nonchalant heroism to work on the screen, the film really needed a witty script and a witty relationship with his German captive. Neither was provided.

Ill Met By Moonlight was war as played by amateur soldiers, ex-public schoolboys, enjoying a practical joke. It was all a bit of a lark, money for jam, a game in which nobody got killed.

Dirk Bogarde's quality is known to us all and here he plays at the very top of his form.   PETER BURNUP *News of the World*

Dirk Bogarde's polite and restrained 'heroic' style is here somewhat over-indulged.   *Monthly Film Bulletin*

As a gentlemanly swashbuckler, Bogarde exploits a rather laid-back charm.
PHILIP OAKES *Evening Standard*

Dirk's performance is a fine, intelligent piece of work.
ANTHONY CARTHEW *Daily Herald*

directed by
Michael Powell and
Emeric Pressburger
U.S. title:
Night Ambush

OPPOSITE
Marius Goring and
Dirk Bogarde in
Ill Met By Moonlight.

BELOW
Dirk Bogarde in
Ill Met By Moonlight.

DOCTOR AT LARGE 1957

directed by
Ralph Thomas

octor at Large, though better than *Doctor at Sea,* was the same old medicine: an unexacting prescription of romance and slapstick in which Dr Simon Sparrow, with ambitions to be a surgeon and work in Sir Lancelot Spratt's butcher shop, takes on a number of temporary posts up and down the country.

The screenplay was a series of disconnected, innocuous and not very funny episodes which leaned heavily on Bogarde's charm plus a well-known character actor in every role, however small.

It was left, as usual, to James Robertson Justice ('I do not growl like a bear, I roar like a lion') to give the film some bite, not least when he was explaining to his colleagues how to cook spaghetti, while he was operating on a patient.

Bogarde acted with a light and bemused touch, slipping with ease into one of those little scenes (comforting a woman who was about to have an operation) which were designed to prove that Sparrow had a vocation and was not just a nice, sweet guy who boobed all the time.

One of the more pleasant boobs was when he took seriously a crank who said he had been coughing up nuts and bolts, and dragged Spratt from his bed in the middle of the night to the operating theatre, only to find the man producing an umbrella from under the sheets and claiming that he had coughed that up as well.

George Coulouris, Richard Gordon,
Terence Longdon, James Robertson Justice
and Dirk Bogarde in *Doctor at Large.*

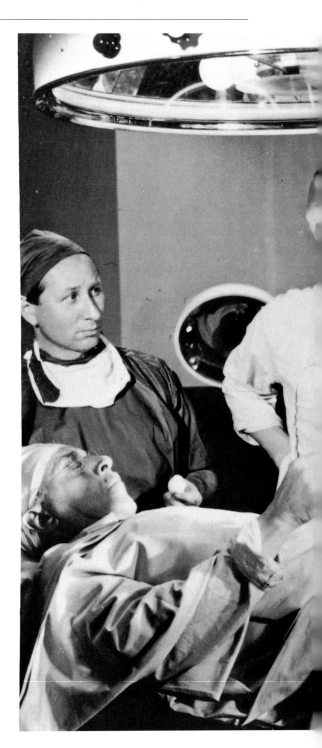

70

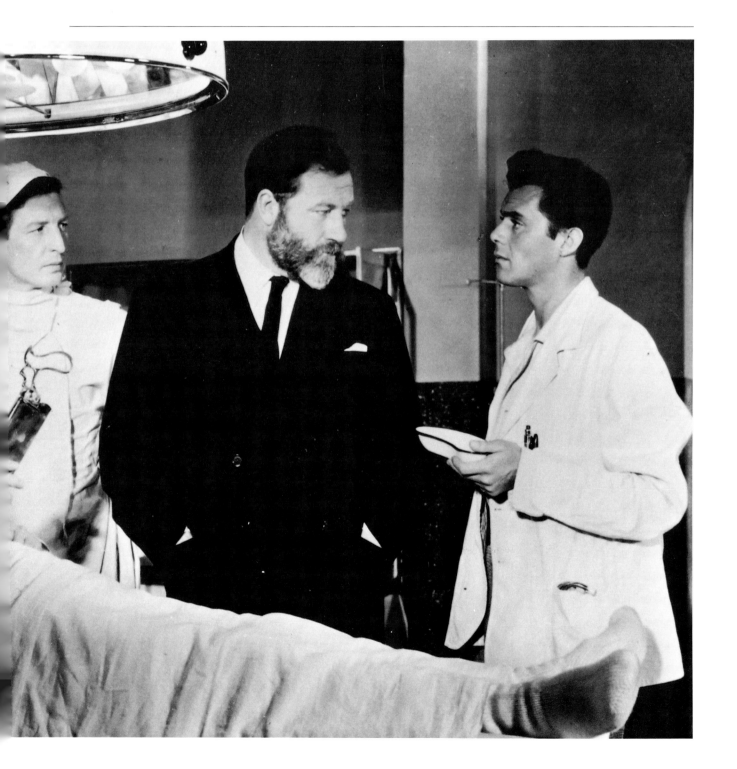

Dirk Bogarde and
Barbara Murray in
Doctor at Large.

Dirk Bogarde, as the young GP, gives his best comic performance yet, persuasive, witty, authoritative.

DILYS POWELL *Sunday Times*

And once again all Mr Bogarde's unforced charm, his quiet and grave approach to hilarity have more appeal than all the gags strung together.

HAROLD CONWAY *Daily Sketch*

The series which began as a healthy romp about medical students is now scraping the floor of the operating theatre for its comic material.

MILTON SHULMAN *Sunday Express*

I know they are not great works of art, but they are enormous fun to make and have a vast family audience appeal. They are entertaining, which, after all, is the essence of my job. They have taught me the main essentials about comedy, and playing and timing for a cinema audience. If it were not for Dr Sparrow, I probably would not be where I am today. For that, and the foresight of producer Betty Box, who practically forced me to play in the first of the series, I shall be for ever grateful.

DIRK BOGARDE *Films and Filming*

Campbell's *Kingdom* set out to compete with Hollywood on its own action-packed territory, indulging in an orgy of rough stuff, playing with fire, oil, dynamite and flood.

The schoolboy adventure was set in Canada. Bogarde played an extremely healthy invalid who climbs every mountain, fords every stream, and plunges into the maelstrom to save the villain (Stanley Baker) from drowning. Nobody was surprised to learn that his English doctor had made a wrong diagnosis.

The film was shot in Italy with the Dolomites standing in for the Rockies (only a Dolomite would have known the difference). The scenery, even when obviously only a backcloth, proved a formidable rival for the actors, most of whom were embarrassingly wooden. The script was so cliché-ridden as to be a parody of the genre, while the direction was so

directed by
Ralph Thomas

Stanley Baker,
Barbara Murray and
Dirk Bogarde in
Campbell's Kingdom.

Betty E. Box,
Ralph Thomas,
Michael Craig and
Dirk Bogarde
on the set of
Campbell's Kingdom.

pedestrian there was no tension.

Surprisingly, there were some critics who thought *Campbell's Kingdom* offered Bogarde his best part in years and that his sensitive, low-key performance would give his career a new lease of life; the truth was that the part was non-existent and the sensitive, low-key performance was totally out of place. There was no tough guy under the gentle, charming, wry fatalism. Far from suggesting a man who had come to claim his inheritance and could, as he threatened, smash the burly Canadians' teeth to the backs of their heads, he looked more like an actor modelling a new line in natty lumberjack shirts.

The final scene, in which everybody else scrambles to safety while he alone rushes round, quite unnecessarily, warning that the dam is about to burst, was only fractionally less absurd than an earlier scene in which he and Michael Craig were discussing some technical matters and it was obvious that neither actor had the faintest idea what he was talking about.

Mr Bogarde is a very good actor with immense personal charm. For years he has been Britain's most popular screen actor, during which time he has never appeared in a good film. This is an interesting phenomenon and it could be deduced that his enormous public prefer to see him in mediocre films. However, as they have never been given the opportunity to see him in anything else, it is impossible to prove this.

JOHN OSBORNE *Evening Standard*

One can imagine the frozen faces with which most players would gallop through. But Mr Bogarde is too honourable an actor for that. Never casual, never playing down, he even succeeds in giving the part authority.   DILYS POWELL *Sunday Times*

As the displaced, determined but bookish Briton who takes on all those odds and muscular characters, Dirk Bogarde appears to be a man who would be more at ease in Mayfair than among the tough roughians of the Rockies.

A. H. WEILER *New York Times*

OPPOSITE
Dirk Bogarde and
Stanley Baker in
Campbell's Kingdom.

A TALE OF TWO CITIES   1958

directed by
Ralph Thomas

A *Tale of Two Cities* has often been staged and filmed. It should have been the best of times, but, with Ralph Thomas directing, it was the worst of times. His plodding studio-bound production lacked life and colour, and was, with rare exceptions, badly acted.

What the romantic melodrama needed was the poetic sweep and verve of Abel Gance to do full justice to the famous set-pieces: the storming of the Bastille, the two trials and the last journey to the guillotine. The latter, as filmed here, was merely a pretty drive in a tumbril through picturesque extras.

There was a great deal of dialogue and far too little cinema. The key scene in which a child is trampled to death under the wheels of an aristocrat's carriage was bungled. Only the peacock's violent reaction to the murder of the Marquis St Evremonde showed any visual awareness.

Sydney Carton's self-sacrifice is probably the most celebrated self-sacrifice in nineteenth-century English fiction. Bogarde, wearing his clothes well, cut an elegant figure and looked handsomely wan and wistful as the love-sick, drunken wastrel. His performance, however, was so lacking in dramatic energy and purpose that Carton made little impression. Carton was, in fact, noticeable only because he was Bogarde. The dissipation and moroseness were not

Stephen Murray, Dorothy Tutin, Dirk Bogarde and Athene Seyler in *A Tale of Two Cities*.

OPPOSITE
Dirk Bogarde in
A Tale of Two Cities.

convincing. The self-absorbing self-pity was there; but the pathos of a wasted life was missing. He did not come into his own until right at the end of the picture when he was in prison dictating his last letter to Lucie Manette (Dorothy Tutin).

The final speech (a voice-over) was beautifully delivered, though many people would have been surprised to learn that only the very last much-quoted line was actually by Dickens; the rest was by the scriptwriter, T.E.B. Clarke.

This is one of his finest performances to date.   LEONARD MOSLEY *Daily Express*

Dirk Bogarde makes no try at the high heroic style. It is quizzical and reserved; so candid and clear-eyed that one finds it hard to take his wallow in the cups quite seriously. I think it will be liked, and rightly so, for Mr Bogarde is an honest actor. But I doubt if it's enough to make this *Tale of Two Cities* the great screen romance of all time, or to efface memories of Martin Harvey and *The Only Way*.

C.A. LEJEUNE *Observer*

Paul Guers and Dirk Bogarde in *A Tale of Two Cities*.

Dirk Bogarde misses much of the suave cynicism of Sydney Carton.

MILTON SHULMAN *Sunday Express*

As Sydney Carton, that almost improbable character, he gives a highly sensitive performance. It is, I think, a far, far better thing than he has ever done.

IVOR ADAMS *Star*

Dorothy Tutin and Dirk Bogarde in *A Tale of Two Cities*.

THE WIND CANNOT READ 1958

**directed by
Ralph Thomas**

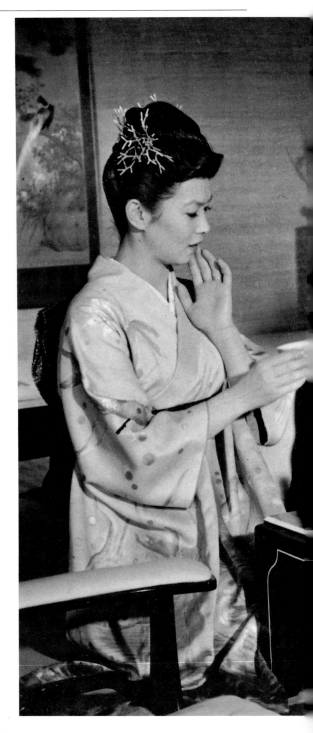

The Wind Cannot Read, a sentimental wartime romance in India, was no *Madam Butterfly*. The film offered quick and uninterestingly photographed trips round the Taj Mahal and other tourist attractions. The scenery was never used imaginatively; it was merely a backcloth, as exciting as a postcard.

Bogarde played a British officer who marries in secret a very wistful and very sad Japanese girl (Yoko Tani), his teacher at the Language School at the Red Fort in New Delhi, before he goes off to fight in Burma where he is captured and tortured. He escapes to come back just in time to see her die of an incurable brain disease, her death conveniently shirking the problem which the film had raised about mixed marriages.

The love affair was handled with such British cinematic tact that when Bogarde was smoking the obligatory post-coital cigarette, he was not only fully clothed but jacket-belted as well, and the sole indication that he had been to bed was that she had changed her dress.

The wind cannot read; and on the evidence of this script, she cannot write either. It was a measure of Bogarde's skill with the clichés that the maladroit screenplay worked at all. His charm and sincerity were invaluable throughout. He was defeated only by the extraneous war scenes. The prologue, where he and John Fraser pretended most unconvincingly to be two lone survivors in the retreat from Burma, was straight out of *Beau Geste*. His escape from the Japs was so improbable as to be silly; while the long walk back to base, in the blazing sun, was *The Four Feathers* all over again without Ralph Richardson.

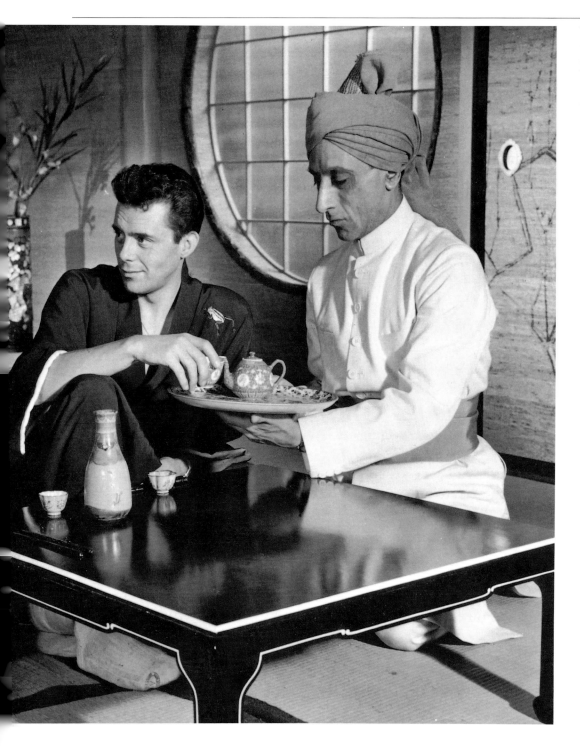

Yoko Tani,
Dirk Bogarde and
Marne Maitland in
*The Wind Cannot
Read*.

John Fraser and
Dirk Bogarde in
*The Wind Cannot
Read*.

Well, this time he shows that he has grown up. To all his old charm he has added manliness, strength, spine, backbone, muscle – call it what you will.

LEONARD MOSLEY *Daily Express*

In this film, where fire, virility, and a positive attack on the cliché officer type are demanded, he still offers too much of the wry smile, the imperceptibly quivering stiff upper lip, the spaniel pathos in the eyes. He is still prowling the screen, demanding mother love from his millions of female fans. Bogarde is honest, sincere, intelligent. But in a film of tragic passion and contemporary significance that is not enough.   DEREK MONSEY *Sunday Express*

He is a reliable but hardly outstanding actor. Comedy seems to suit him best and, on the evidence of the present experiment, high passion least.

JYMPSON HARMAN *Evening News*

Bogarde exerts his particular kind of lazy charm in a way that should make every woman yearn to darn his socks. But the film is Yoko Tani's triumph.

RONALD HIGHAM *Daily Sketch*

Dirk Bogarde's flight lieutenant is easily the best thing he has done.

MATTHEW NORGATE *Manchester Guardian*

The best screen performance of his screen career.   *The Times*

*J*ezabel, a strident and immature *pièce noire*, written in 1932, but not published until 1948, had its English première at Oxford.

The play, generally thought to be one of Anouilh's worst, is a wildly melodramatic account of an unhappy son in love with an heiress but so humiliated by his poverty and vulgar parents that he longs to be an orphan.

As the son Dirk Bogarde gives a competent acting performance with conscious grace and good looks, but hell and torment are needed.

J.B. BOOTHROYD *Punch*

Dirk Bogarde, who has one expression that is grave and weak, another that is grave and wry, and a capacity for sudden shouting that serves to break the monotony, rings what changes he can on limited acting resources.

KENNETH TYNAN *Observer*

Mr Bogarde plays Marc with a fine nervous fire, and it is the play's fault and not his that his moral capitulation at the end seems an unconvincing conclusion to be drawn from a few scattered hints about his capacities for debauch.　　*The Times*

a play by
Jean Anouilh
directed by
Frank Hauser
The Playhouse,
Oxford

Dirk Bogarde and
Hermione Baddeley
in *Jezabel*.

THE DOCTOR'S DILEMMA   1959

directed by
Anthony Asquith

Life does not cease to be funny when people die any more than it ceases to be serious when people laugh.

BERNARD SHAW

Shaw wrote *The Doctor's Dilemma*, a dry and cynical comedy at the expense of the medical profession, in answer to a challenge that it was impossible to write a funny death-bed scene.

The actual dilemma is very artificial. An eminent surgeon (John Robinson) can only perform one operation. Whose life shall he save? The life of an honest, decent, very ordinary man? Or the life of a rotten blackguard who happens to be a painter of genius? Since the surgeon is infatuated with the painter's wife (Leslie Caron), he decides to operate on the decent man, hoping (rightly, as it turns out) that if the genius is left to the bungling hands of his colleagues he will die.

In the theatre, the dilemma is less interesting than the doctors themselves. The saddest thing about Anthony Asquith's film (hardly a film, merely a photographed play) was that the doctors who should have provided so much of the civilised wit were diminished, subdued and not funny. Many of their best lines had been cut.

The emphasis was on the artist. Bogarde's amoral Dubedat ('I don't believe in morality') had all the charm and all the cheek. He was especially good when he was justifying his conduct to the outraged doctors; and what was so good about the performance was that he did not attempt to disguise that underneath all the charm and impudent wit Dubedat was an unpleasant and vicious scoundrel.

Robert Morley,
Felix Aylmer,
Alastair Sim,
Dirk Bogarde and
John Robinson in
The Doctor's Dilemma.

His moving death-bed scene would have been even more moving if the famous credo ('I believe in Michelangelo, Velázquez and Rembrandt; in the might of design, the mystery of colour, the redemption of all things by Beauty ever-lasting, and the message of Art that has made these hands blessed. Amen, amen') had not been edited and mumbled.

This sometimes wilful and often wasted actor takes to a worthwhile part like the real actor he is.

DEREK MONSEY *Sunday Express*

Dirk Bogarde free from the tyranny of not particularly rewarding parts puts up the finest performance of his career as Dubedat.

PETER BURNUP *News of the World*

Outstandingly the best in every way, Dirk Bogarde, as the dying artist, brings a much-needed breath of life to the film.

NINA HIBBIN *Daily Worker*

Bogarde plays the doomed part with astonishing brilliance.   IVOR ADAMS *Star*

Dirk Bogarde's Dubedat is rather too mild and bland in his scene of insolent self-justification. But the death-scene contains the most moving and the most deeply felt playing the actor has given us on the screen.   DILYS POWELL *Sunday Times*

Dirk Bogarde, of course, is more than a fashionable star; he is a serious actor of talent and strength of character. The bias of his personality is towards sincerity and honesty – that is, his quiet, assured manner of speech and the directness of his eye are pointers on the screen to fundamental trustworthiness.

ROGER MANVELL *Films and Filming*

Mr Bogarde's painter is the best and most difficult thing he has ever done.

PAUL DEHN *News Chronicle*

Anatole de Grunwald, Anthony Asquith and Dirk Bogarde on the set of *The Doctor's Dilemma*.

ABOVE AND LEFT
Dirk Bogarde and
Leslie Caron in
The Doctor's Dilemma.

LIBEL 1959

directed by
Anthony Asquith

Olivia de Havilland,
Robert Morley and
Dirk Bogarde in *Libel*.

*L*ibel was a very conventional pre-war courtroom drama, updated to the fifties, in which a rich baronet accused of being an imposter goes to law to defend himself only to find he is also accused of attempted murder.

The courtroom exchanges (despite the author being a distinguished barrister and despite the comic personae of Robert Morley and Wilfrid Hyde-White as leading counsels) were exceptionally dull, lacking the sharp wit which had made Otto Preminger's recently released *Anatomy of Murder* so exciting. Morley's glib theatrics and Hyde-White's light-weight performance actually got in the way, and the film

was certainly not helped by a silly denouement, in which the verdict having finally gone in his favour, the baronet takes back the wife (Olivia de Havilland) who had ditched him in open court and thanks his false accuser.

The film offered Bogarde the opportunity to play three roles: the silver-haired baronet suffering from amnesia (I CAN'T REMEMBER! he screams from the witness box in his best hysterical manner); his double, a third-rate repertory actor; and a surprise witness, a silent wreck of a man called Number Fifteen, who is quite visibly the camp actor under a heavy make-up.

Dirk Bogarde in *Libel*.

When you see him on the set, you realise he's got two faces. The left side of his face can look strong and the right side can look weak. When he appears in Libel *as the aristocratic strong character, we photographed the left side. When he was the weak character, it was the right side. As Number Fifteen, he doesn't speak, it's largely make-up.*

ANTHONY ASQUITH quoted by
ERNEST BETTS *People*

BELOW AND RIGHT
Dirk Bogarde in his
three roles in *Libel*.

Dirk Bogarde in *Libel* plays himself, and his double – and gives the performance of his career so far.

JOHN WATERMAN *Evening Standard*

There's really not much in the film apart from Mr Bogarde's most subtle and clever differentiation between the baronet and the envious chip-on-shoulder actor.

RICHARD MALLETT *Punch*

Mr Bogarde's own performance is in the Guinness class.

PAUL DEHN *News Chronicle*

SONG WITHOUT END 1960

directed by
Charles Vidor
and George Cukor

Bogarde made his Hollywood debut in *Song Without End*, which was directed by Charles Vidor until he died of a heart-attack in the middle of the shooting and George Cukor had to take over. The film purported to describe the recitals and loves of Franz Liszt, a virtuoso on the concert platform and in bed, and was a companion piece to *A Song to Remember*, in which Cornel Wilde played Chopin.

The script, a superficial mix of romantic twaddle and vulgar exhibitionism, showed the composer at war with himself, torn between two careers, music and religion. The film limited itself, with un-Hollywood-like economy, to just two affairs. No excesses were spared in other departments, the material for the costumes alone being sufficient to cover *two* football fields.

The two women were the Countess Marie d'Agoult and Carolyne zu Sayn-Wittgenstein, played by Genevieve Page and Capucine respectively. Capucine, one of France's top models, who had never acted before, and certainly didn't look as if she intended to start, restricted herself to modelling clothes and jewellery. She looked as if she had been carved out of alabaster, cold, monumental and quite in-animate. The acting was left to Martita Hunt, who had no difficulty whatsoever in conveying the breeding and good taste of the Grand Duchess of Weimar.

One of the major pleasures was the brief yet hilarious glimpse of the first perform-ance of *Lohengrin*. Additional amusements included Liszt, Chopin and Georges Sand walking the streets late at night singing *Sur Le Pont D'Avignon*. ('We look like characters out of a bad opera,' said one wag.) There

Dirk Bogarde in
Song Without End.

93

was also that scene — equally dear to American movie-biogs — when Liszt drags the piano out of the house and into the courtyard to play the *Hungarian Rhapsody*, to the delight of the happy villagers, who all carry on as if they were in *The White Horse Inn*. Best of all was the sight of the composer, in the middle of a performance of *Lohengrin*, suddenly distracted by his mistress's absence and forgetting to conduct, an incident which passes totally unnoticed by the members of the orchestra.

Song Without End (originally called *Crescendo*) was no *Hungarian Rhapsody* for Bogarde, who found on his arrival in America that contrary to what he had been promised in London, he was expected to play the piano. Initially he had to go through hell trying to master the keyboard. But he mastered it so well that when the film was finally released audiences, watching his hands pounding the keys, were full of admiration for his virtuoso synchronisation. It was a very impressive feat, and rightly highly praised.

Dirk Bogarde and Genevieve Page in *Song Without End*.

Mr Dirk Bogarde's work at the keyboard is splendidly convincing, but though Mr Bogarde is a pleasant and graceful actor, he does not convey the sensational amalgam of genius, generosity, charlatanism, gargantuan sensuality and religiosity that we find in Liszt's biographies. *The Times*

Though his strength is in the nuance rather than the firework, Dirk Bogarde makes a reasonably tempestuous Liszt.

FRED MAJDALANY *Daily Mail*

It is as near a portrait of a genius as any actor probably can get.

ALEXANDER WALKER *Evening Standard*

Dirk Bogarde plays Franz Liszt with a heavy-lidden petulance utterly in keeping with the magnificent banality of the script; we have not seen this kind of random eyebrow-raising and facial twitching, designed I suppose to convey creative neurosis, since Miss Jennifer Jones' last picture.   CLANCY SIGAL *Time and Tide*

THE SINGER NOT THE SONG 1961

directed by
Roy Baker

OPPOSITE
Dirk Bogarde in *The Singer Not The Song*.

BELOW
Dirk Bogarde,
Laurence Naismith
and John Mills in *The Singer Not The Song*.

The Singer Not The Song was a gay Mexican western about a bad bandit and a good priest. Their relationship was either spiritual with homosexual undertones or homosexual with spiritual undertones; it depended where the audience was looking at the time.

Bogarde was the bandit Anacleto, a cardboard and novelletish villain in drag, who hates the Church but loves the priest (hence the title). He sounded very English, and he certainly looked very English, surrounded by henchmen and extras all of a swarthier and darker hue.

He was dressed or rather *sheathed* all in black: black sombrero, black shirt, black gloves, black leather pants, riding a white horse, and carrying a whip and a white

pussy-cat, looking for all the world, as *The Times* critic observed, 'like a latterday Queen Kelly' – who, it will be remembered, wore only a pussy-cat. His black shiny leather pants, so tight they looked as if they had been sprayed on, were much admired.

The Singer Not The Song is one of the screen's great unconsummated love affairs (though only the bandit knows this) and the final shoot-out – a mixture of B-movie and nineteenth-century opera, more lust in the dust than *Duel in the Sun* – ends with bandit and priest, both shot, locked in mortal embrace, and the bandit squeezing the priest's hand, smiling contentedly, murmuring 'the singer not the song'.

Laurence Naismith, as a drunken bandito, behaved as if he had seen every western since *The Great Train Robbery* and threw himself with great energy all over the set. Even funnier was Philip Green's music, not so much a score as semaphore, and so over the top as to be a parody of itself. Green, unwilling to let go, was still clanging away long after 'The End' had come up.

The Singer Not The Song, lumpishly directed, unsubtly edited, took its time and was often at a loss how to fill a cinemascope screen. What the story really needed was a treatment and script by Graham Greene and both actors aware of the homosexual sub-text. John Mills, who played the priest, seemed to be acting in a different film to Bogarde.

Bogarde thought the priest should have been very young, very innocent, very beautiful and that Anacleto should have been a real villain driving around in an old chevrolet, not a caricature of evil on a white horse.

The real star of *Singer* is a pair of trousers, jeans-type. They are of black, lustrous leather. They shine with a distinction which is absent in every other department of this misbegotten film, including direction (Roy Baker) and script (Nigel Balchin).   CLANCY SIGAL *Daily Express*

What matters more in *The Singer Not The Song* are the performances not the picture. They are endurable and often enjoyable – especially Mr Bogarde, whose each scene is a victory over his costume designer.
                    ALEXANDER WALKER *Evening Standard*

Dirk Bogarde and John Mills in *The Singer Not The Song*.

LA SPOSA BELLA 1961

directed by
Nunnally Johnson
English title:
The Angel Wore Red

*T*he *Angel Wore Red*, set during the Spanish Civil War, was about an unfrocked priest, a cabaret entertainer and a missing holy relic.

Dirk Bogarde plays the priest with skill and restraint, in a performance that is consistently in key.

EUGENE ARCHER *New York Times*

Larking around as a fallen priest with Ava Gardner is all very well when you're still a young man. But when you're turning forty you want to do slightly more serious things.

DIRK BOGARDE quoted by
THOMAS WISEMAN *Evening Standard*

Bogarde's next film was *Victim*.

Ava Gardner and
Dirk Bogarde in
The Angel Wore Red.

Joseph Cotten and
Dirk Bogarde in
The Angel Wore Red.

PART TWO

INTERNATIONAL STAR

Dirk Bogarde in *Victim*, 1961

VICTIM 1961

directed by
Basil Dearden

This new film may shock my nice young doctor public, but you can't go on making films just to please your fans. You can't leave all the adult films to the French, Italian and Swedes.

DIRK BOGARDE quoted by
CECIL WILSON *Daily Mail*

When Bogarde appeared in *Victim*, a gripping little blackmailing thriller directed with plenty of pace and made less routine by the victims all being homosexuals, the English Press acknowledged the risk he was taking with his career, the public in general, his female fans in particular, and they applauded his courage.

In 1960 in nine out of ten cases of blackmail in Great Britain the victims were homosexual. *Victim*, in criticising the then-existing law, was repeating what the Wolfenden Report had already recommended in 1957: namely that a law which sends homosexuals to prison was a charter for blackmail and that what consenting adults did in private was their own business. The film helped to change the law.

Bogarde played a homosexual barrister who risks his career and marriage to break an extortion racket when his young friend, a wages clerk on a building site, commits suicide rather than implicate him. The blackmailer, all in leather, dark glasses, and riding a motor bike, turned out (so a print of Michelangelo's David on the wall of his flat implied) to be homosexual himself, though why he didn't blackmail the barrister rather than the clerk was never clear.

Bogarde gave a thoughtful, intelligent, tactful performance. The script was careful not to outrage and alienate the audience. It

Sylvia Syms and
Dirk Bogarde in
Victim.

Dirk Bogarde and
Donald Churchill in
Victim.

was at pains to establish that though he was a practising lawyer he was not a practising homosexual; that he had been only emotionally, not sexually, involved with the young man; and that he had stopped seeing him the moment he had wanted him.

Bogarde held the film together, providing a solid centre, while the well-chosen supporting cast acted a cross-section of victims drawn from every class, all sincere mouthpieces for reform, and not a camp fellow among them. The only obvious homosexual turned out to be a policeman, *un agent provocateur*.

Inevitably there were those who reproached the makers for tackling the problem in too superficial a manner; but the script was pretty frank for its time and certainly it discussed its subject with far more realism than most people had expected.

The American censor refused *Victim* his seal of approval, finding the film 'thematically objectionable' and insisting that 'sexual aberration could only be suggested and not actually spelled out'.

To treat the theme as a thriller may not be particularly brave, but to treat it at all was brave.   DILYS POWELL *Sunday Times*

He risks curdling the adulation of his fans. But I predict that his brave, sensitive picture of an unhappy, terribly bewildered man will win him and this film a far wider audience.

ALEXANDER WALKER *Evening Standard*

In accepting this part, Mr Bogarde took a brave, calculated risk. What he may lose in terms of teenage adulation, he is sure to gain in adult respect for a performance that is intelligent and accomplished.

THOMAS WISEMAN *Sunday Express*

But what seems at first an attack on extortion seems at last a coyly sensational exploitation of homosexuality as a theme –

and what's more offensive, an implicit approval of homosexuality as a practice. Almost all the deviates in the film are fine fellows – well dressed, well spoken, sensitive, kind. The only one who acts like an overt invert turns out to be a detective. Everybody in the picture who disapproves of homosexuals proves to be an ass, a dolt or a sadist. Nowhere does the film suggest that homosexuality is a serious (but often curable) neurosis that attacks the biological basis of life itself. 'I can't help the way I am,' says one of the sodomites in this movie. 'Nature played me a dirty trick.' And the scriptwriters, whose psychiatric information is clearly coeval with the statute they dispute, accept the sick-silly self-delusion as a medical fact.

Time Magazine

Anthony Nicholls, Dennis Price and Dirk Bogarde in *Victim*.

H.M.S. DEFIANT   1962

The year 1962 saw the release not only of *H.M.S. Defiant* but also *Billy Budd* and the re-make of *Mutiny on the Bounty* with Marlon Brando and Trevor Howard. So it was a life on the ocean wave, then: press-gangs, rum, buggery, maggoty cheese, cat-o'-nine tails, and gory battles. What more could any self-respecting eighteenth-century sailor want?

H.M.S. Defiant, a schoolboy naval yarn in the Captain Marryat/C.S. Forester manner, was set during the Napoleonic wars and described the sort of events which led to the Spithead Mutiny in 1797.

Alec Guinness was cast as a humane commander of a frigate. Bogarde was his sadistic first lieutenant ('a future Drake with a vicious streak and a silver spoon') who had powerful friends in the Admiralty and had made a career by getting his superior officers court-martialled for breaches of regulations. The story developed into their personal duel for supremacy.

'There's not an ounce of charm in this character,' Bogarde explained to Cecil Wilson of the *Daily Mail*. 'He never even smiles except possibly when he sees a choice piece of flogging.' The lieutenant was never happier than when he was having the captain's twelve-year-old midshipman son flogged daily.

Critics and audiences were divided as to which actor gave the best performance. Bogarde, acting with smooth, handsome, smirking insolence, screaming *you mutinous filth!*, and ending with a richly deserved knife in his chest, certainly had the more showy part.

The battle scenes were spectacular and brutal.

directed by
Lewis Gilbert
U.S. title:
Damn the Defiant

Dirk Bogarde and
Alec Guinness in
H.M.S. Defiant.

BELOW
Victor Maddern,
Anthony Quayle,
Murray Melvin and
Dirk Bogarde in
H.M.S. Defiant.

Guinness's role in this film is so decent, and so dull that he is engulfed in his rival star's welter of villainy.

LEONARD MOSLEY *Daily Express*

Dirk Bogarde does extremely well as the suave bully, but as was to be expected, much the greater authority, distinction and personality is in Alec Guinness's captain.

Guardian

It is rather the sort of film one could imagine being screened before the morning runs every day at Gordonstoun.

PENELOPE GILLIATT *Observer*

OPPOSITE
Dirk Bogarde, Alec Guinness and Maurice Denham in *H.M.S. Defiant*.

THE PASSWORD IS COURAGE   1962

directed by
Andrew L. Stone

The Password is Courage, which was based on the escapades and escapes of Sergeant-Major Charles Coward in the Second World War, was the latest (very late) in a long line of British POW films stretching back to the stiff-upper-lip, quasi-documentary days of *The Captive Heart*. The barbed wire, watch towers and wooden huts all seemed dreadfully familiar.

The screenplay, a very tall story, evidently mainly true (though it never seemed so), concentrated on comedy rather than excitement, and recounted a series of pranks played on the silly Germans. 'Do you take us for idiots?' screamed the commandant. The answer was frankly yes. The officers (represented by Reginald Beckwith) and the guards (represented by Colin Blakely) had no reality; they were there strictly for the laughs.

The POWs had such a jolly war they might have been at Butlin's. There was one particularly funny sequence in which they set fire to the whole camp and rushed around, fuelling the flames and generally behaving as if they were all in a Keystone Kops film.

The final escape was the cheekiest of them all, with Coward and a fellow prisoner (Alfred Lynch) driving through the enemy lines on a fire-engine, clanging away, and the advancing German troops getting off the road to let them pass.

The acknowledgement that things were not so much fun at Auschwitz, which admittedly was in the original book (and which must have brought back terrible memories to Bogarde, who had entered Belsen at the end of the war) nevertheless seemed grossly out of place in all the farce. When the film was shown on television, the scenes were cut.

Bogarde was not well cast as Coward. It wasn't so much that he was officer rather than sergeant-major material and that the cockney accent came and went, but that he wasn't believable in any of the situations.

BELOW AND OPPOSITE
Dirk Bogarde and
Alfred Lynch in
The Password is Courage.

Dirk Bogarde plays Charlie Coward with a debonair touch which somehow misses the man-of-the-people qualities of the real man.
LEONARD MOSLEY *Daily Express*

Dirk Bogarde gives a breezy relaxed performance as Coward.
NINA HIBBIN *Daily Worker*

Dirk Bogarde plays the hero with charm and fluency.   *Guardian*

THE MIND BENDERS 1963

directed by
Basil Dearden

The Mind Benders, based on recent American experiments on the effects of prolonged isolation on the central nervous system, got a rough time from the critics, most finding it more mind-boggling than mind-bending.

In his autobiography Bogarde claims that the film was ahead of its time. But the objections had nothing to do with the brain-washing; John Frankenheimer's *The Manchurian Candidate*, which dealt with exactly the same subject, and far more excitingly, had just come out and was enjoying a critical and popular success. The

objection was to the treatment. Michael Relph and Basil Dearden would have been better advised to have stuck to the social-thriller formula which had served them so well in *Sapphire* (dealing with racial prejudice), *Victim* (homosexuality) and *Life for Ruth* (Jehovah Witnesses). Instead they opted for a silly women's-magazine approach.

Bogarde played an Oxford physiologist who, at the request of British intelligence, takes part in an unlikely experiment in a water-tank in which he is deprived of sight, smell, sound, touch and taste for eight

Mary Ure and
Dirk Bogarde in
The Mind Benders.

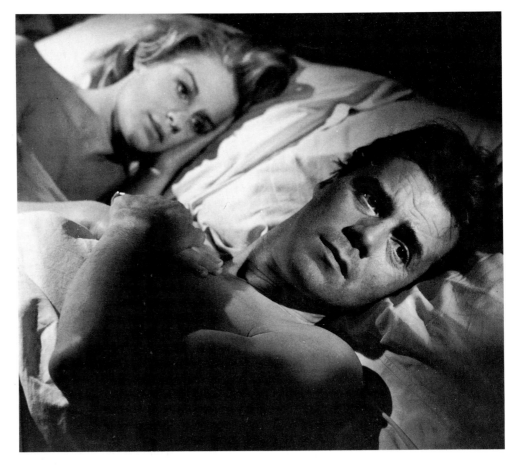

hours in order to prove whether an elderly colleague who has committed suicide was either a traitor knowingly selling secrets to the enemy or merely a zombie.

It was impossible to take the story seriously. The intelligence officer (played by John Clements, who sounded like Noël Coward and even on occasions looked like him) gets a research assistant (Michael Bryant) to persuade the physiologist that he no longer loves his wife (Mary Ure) and then does not bother either to inform the wife or keep her under observation.

Bogarde was at his best, just out of the tank, totally disorientated, clinging like a frightened child to Michael Bryant, and at his happiest at the end delivering a baby (evidently the perfect cure for indoctrination) in a scene which would have been more appropriate as a climax to one of his *Doctor* films. In between, looking very tired, he was to be seen doing a lot of acting, and generally being beastly to his wife in a self-indulgently theatrical manner which recalled an earlier stage in his career.

How this young man is horribly brain-washed, purely for security reasons (and in the process estranged from his loving wife); how he is brought back to humanity by attending her in childbirth (a brisk ten-minute labour) makes a stunning story, not to be missed by any connoisseur of the nasty or the absurd.

PATRICK GIBBS *Daily Telegraph*

This film belongs, to quote yet another remark from the film, 'strictly to Frankenstein country' and it is a pretty shabby and sordid example of the genre.

LEONARD MOSLEY *Daily Express*

Dirk Bogarde in *The Mind Benders*.

BELOW
John Clements, Michael Bryant and Dirk Bogarde in *The Mind Benders*.

I *Could Go On Singing* (they should have stuck to the original title – *The Lonely Stage*) was a tear-jerking vehicle for Judy Garland's comeback; the film paralleled Garland's career so often that it seemed as if she were re-enacting her own life.

She played a world-famous American singer, a neurotic, self-destructive, vulnerable woman, who had put her career before her marriage and left her lover to bring up their child (charmingly acted by Gregory Phillips). Her performance, occasionally touching a raw nerve, was hailed as a triumph over a corny, old-fashioned, saccharine-sweet script.

Bogarde played the resentful lover, a Harley Street surgeon, skilfully and self-effacingly, giving her noble support throughout and especially in the scene in the hospital (which he had written in three days and rehearsed with her for six hours), where he persuades her that she owes it to her impatient, hand-clapping Palladium audience to turn up. So convinced were some critics by Garland's acting they presumed she must have been ad-libbing.

Bogarde himself had one good scene in the back of a car: 'I am so sick with anger I can hardly speak to you... You're an egocentric, grasping bitch.' Elsewhere their quarrelling was only melodramatic.

I Could Go On Singing, with its badly staged musical numbers, would have been a lot more interesting if, instead of half-cashing-in on the legend, the script could have been based on her actual behaviour on and off the set.

directed by
Ronald Neame

Gregory Phillips and Dirk Bogarde in *I Could Go On Singing*.

OPPOSITE
Judy Garland and Dirk Bogarde in *I Could Go On Singing*.

Bogarde, cast as Garland's former lover, has a role which seems to have been devalued somewhere along the line, reducing the character almost to that of a straightman cueing in his co-star to her complex of emotions. This Bogarde does with an unfailing unobtrusive tact, but it is not a role of much content.

RICHARD WHITEHALL *Films and Filming*

Dirk Bogarde and Judy Garland in *I Could Go On Singing*.

In a most self-effacing performance Bogarde lends the story his particular brand of steady sincerity.

FELIX BARKER *Evening News*

Mr Bogarde gives one of those deceptively unassuming performances whose diffidence conceals a desire to help Miss Garland act more movingly than she has ever acted before.

PAUL DEHN *Daily Herald*

Dirk Bogarde, burdened with the chilling role of the aloof and pompous father... warms him with his own emotional finesse into a human being.

CECIL WILSON *Daily Mail*

directed by
Ralph Thomas

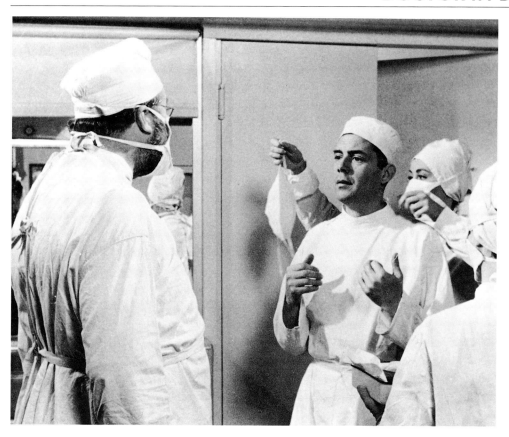

octor in Distress was the fifth Doctor film and Bogarde made it to make himself some money after *The Mind Benders* had flopped and in case *The Servant* flopped too.

The doctor in distress was not Simon Sparrow but Sir Lancelot Spratt, now a patient with a slipped disc and but a shadow of his former self, the old bark having given way to a new and boring sentimentality. He was in love with his physiotherapist and walking in his sleep. The man was clearly not Spratt but an imposter.

Bogarde, ostensibly the star, was in a supporting role, while James Robertson Justice looked exactly what he was – a supporting actor elevated to a leading role neither he nor the scriptwriters nor the director could sustain.

The director's touch is light, the acting impeccable, with Dirk Bogarde perfectly at ease as Sparrow.

PATRICK GIBBS *Daily Telegraph*

But when I speak of control I am thinking in particular of Dirk Bogarde. Polish and presence, the timing of comedy and the emphasis of emotion – Mr Bogarde has won an authority which is a constant pleasure to watch.

DILYS POWELL *Sunday Times*

James Robertson Justice and Dirk Bogarde in *Doctor in Distress*.

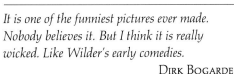

THE SERVANT 1963

It is one of the funniest pictures ever made. Nobody believes it. But I think it is really wicked. Like Wilder's early comedies.

DIRK BOGARDE

directed by
Joseph Losey

The Servant, which arrived in the wake of the Profumo scandal and the Denning Report, was one of the most original films of the 1960s, a key work in the careers of both Joseph Losey and Bogarde.

Harold Pinter's screenplay (based on a short story by Robin Maugham) described the seduction of Tony (James Fox), a young aristocrat, by his manservant Barrett, who uses flattery, pimpery, booze, drugs and perversion. Their intense relationship and reversal of roles was used as a metaphor for the British class-war, their baroque disintegration being mirrored in the disintegration of the elegant Georgian house in which most of the action took place.

The film faltered only in the final, highly stylised orgy. Though the scene was the direct development of all that had gone before, it nevertheless felt gratis; the debauchery provided a Fellini-like coda which was not needed. The story was already over.

Bogarde, on his first appearance, walking to the house in his dark overcoat, spotted scarf, leather gloves and pork pie hat, immediately cut a sinister cat-like figure. Barrett was knowing, cunning and insolent, and never more so than when he was being most deferential. The propriety was always tinged with mocking irony.

The camp northern accent, the fussing around, the sparring with Tony's girl-friend (Wendy Craig), the battle of the flowers, the sado-masochistic ball games on the

Dirk Bogarde,
James Fox,
Hazel Terry and
Wendy Craig in
The Servant.

119

stairs – all were carried off with great wit. There was one memorable close-up of him sitting, all on his own in the kitchen, biting his nails brooding, Iago-like in his malevolence. And yet underneath all the vicious nastiness, the inherent weakness of the man was always visible.

There was an excellent scene in a pub, with master and servant separated by a partition which divided the saloon from the public bar. Barrett, down-and-out, grovelled pathetically, whining for another chance. Barrett could have been (almost certainly was) acting, but the ambiguity of whether he was acting or not in no way negated the insecurity and continuing servility the scene had revealed.

Bogarde's performance won him the British Film Academy's award for the best actor. James Fox as the rich, pampered Tony, indolent, effete and degraded, was the perfect partner.

Dirk Bogarde in *The Servant*.

OPPOSITE
Dirk Bogarde and James Fox in
The Servant.

Mr Bogarde is a great star, but we shall
never be able to forget that he is an actor
to the tips of his fingers as well.

The Times

Dirk Bogarde, as the viciously sissy,
vaguely libidinous manservant, gives a
performance that leaves no doubt that he is
a true actor.

DAVID ROBINSON *Financial Times*

Dirk Bogarde's is a beautifully studied
performance, by far the best of a
distinguished career; watching him is like
being hypnotised by a viper.

LEONARD MOSLEY *Daily Express*

As for Dirk Bogarde's Hugo, he has never
done anything better – a wonderfully
macabre suggestion of a brutal nature
beneath a smooth surface.

PATRICK GIBBS *Daily Telegraph*

But above all it contains the finest
performance yet given by Bogarde, who is
surely the most under-rated of British
actors. He brings to his North Country
manservant a finely controlled blend of
vulgarity and superficial culture.

PETER BAKER *Films and Filming*

OPPOSITE
Dirk Bogarde and
Wendy Craig in
The Servant.

BELOW
Dirk Bogarde and
James Fox in
The Servant.

HOT ENOUGH FOR JUNE   1964

directed by
Ralph Thomas
U.S. title: Agent 8¾

Hot Enough For June, a tepid comedy-thriller, short on comedy and thrills, lacking in style and ingenuity, was a spy spoof, attempting to cash in on James Bond's phenomenal success at the box office in Dr No.

Bogarde played an amateur spy, so amateur that he is recruited through the labour exchange and at first does not even know he is a spy. He falls in love with a beautiful counter-spy, the daughter of an Iron Curtain intelligence chief, and spends his time running round Prague (very unconvincingly impersonated by Padua), disguised as a waiter, Alpine soldier, plumber and milkman. There was one moment of tension at the British Embassy gates, right at the very end, when it seemed as if the gates would never open and the milkman would be arrested.

The British and Communist intelligence officers were played by Robert Morley and Leo McKern, two actors who are quite capable of being jolly and dangerous at the same time, but here they were allowed only to be comic and not nearly comic enough.

Dirk Bogarde wears his disguises amiably, though after *The Servant* one can't but feel he is a little too adult for this statutory role of amiably feckless young adventurer.

Monthly Film Bulletin

Perhaps you think as it's a lighthearted comedy it can do no harm. Now everyone knows that as long as there's a cold-war atmosphere there will be spying and counter-spying. Don't you see that you're only helping to stir things up by adding your contribution (however jolly) to the cold-war legends?

Open Letter to producer BETTY BOX
from NINA HIBBIN *Daily Worker*

Robert Morley,
John Le Mesurier and
Dirk Bogarde in
Hot Enough For June.

OPPOSITE
Dirk Bogarde in
Hot Enough For June.

KING AND COUNTRY 1964

directed by
Joseph Losey

The First World War killed 4,741,609 men. *King and Country* was the story of one man's death at Passchendaele in 1917. Shot in eighteen days on a budget of £80,000, the film was based on John Wilson's stage play *Hamp*, the story of a shell-shocked private, the sole survivor of his original intake, who, unable to take any more, had started walking away from the guns. He was arrested, court-martialled and shot for desertion. ('It is a bit amateur to plead for justice,' said the prosecuting officer.)

Losey opened with a long look at Charles Sargeant Jagger's magnificent frieze on the Royal Artillery Memorial at Hyde Park Corner, a monument celebrating a royal fellowship of death – an ironic start to a story which would end ingloriously in the mud in a bungled execution.

The film thereafter stayed within the confines of the claustrophobic, water-logged, rat-infested trenches, using only very occasionally and most effectively, interpolated stills of famous war photographs and less familiar images of home to establish the outside world.

Bogarde was cast as the officer charged with defending Hamp, a task the officer finds distasteful and accepts with ill-will. The transition from contempt to humanity was not particularly well scripted, relying on the actor to suggest the deepening involvement. (He did it so well that one critic saw a developing homosexual relationship.)

There were some good old-fashioned theatrics in the confrontation between Bogarde and Leo McKern in his role of Medical Officer who refuses to recognize shell-shock, an obnoxious sot many would

126

Leo McKern and
Dirk Bogarde in
King and Country.

Tom Courtenay and
Dirk Bogarde in
King and Country.

have recognised from Wilfred Owen's *War Poetry*.

The most famous scene in the film is the final irony with Hamp apologising for the firing squad having failed to kill him ('Sorry, sir') and the officer, who had pleaded so eloquently for his life, having to finish him off. It was an irony not appreciated by Bedfordshire County Council, who promptly banned the film and refused to lift their ban until the *coup de grâce* was cut.

Bogarde's fine performance wavered only once in an over-extended mime, along the duckboards, when he had to express the officer's physical and mental collapse on hearing Hamp's sentence.

Tom Courtenay, perfect casting for Hamp (though the screenplay made him far too articulate), won the prize for best actor at the Venice Film Festival. There were many who thought the award should have been a joint award for both actors.

It does not matter too much whether one says that Courtenay and Bogarde are superb or that Losey has got superb performances from them; for the audience, the result is the same. It was Tom Courtenay who won the prize for the best actor at Venice, but I am not at all sure that Bogarde is not even better. But this is as futile a question as the previous one. The point is that Losey has built his film on the confrontation of Courtenay and Bogarde; and he, and they, bring it off.

RICHARD ROUD *Guardian*

Equally convincing is Dirk Bogarde – a great screen actor at last finding parts worthy of great acting. He is magnificent.

CLIVE BARNES *Daily Express*

Mr Bogarde's performance with its indications of growing involvement, growing pity, is a fine and a generous one: a self-effacing performance which stands aside to let you see the accused man.

DILYS POWELL *Sunday Times*

And standing out from everything in this fine, stark film – the performances of Dirk Bogarde and Tom Courtenay. Both are outstandingly moving and sensitive.

MICHAEL THORNTON *Sunday Express*

Dirk Bogarde and Tom Courtenay in *King and Country*.

THE HIGH BRIGHT SUN   1965

directed by
Ralph Thomas

Denholm Elliott and
Dirk Bogarde in
The High Bright Sun.

The High Bright Sun, a film about terrorism in Cyprus during the State of Emergency in the late 1950s, managed to make no reference to Turkey or the Turks. 'Well, we wanted to keep politics out of it,' explained the producer Betty E. Box to Felix Barker, critic of the *Evening News*.

Bogarde played a cynical British intelligence officer who correctly suspects his girl-friend, an American archaeologist, of knowing the whereabouts of a guerrilla leader. He was very aggressive with the dialogue, clipping every irony, and generally behaving in such an unpleasant manner to the natives and his superior officer (who had so little to do that he spent most of his time reading *Woman's Own*) that he emerged almost as the villain. The screenplay was so badly constructed that in the film's one exciting sequence, a cross-country man-hunt, he made no appearance.

Susan Strasberg, as his girl-friend, in her white make-up, looked as if she were about to act in a Kabuki drama. The love-interest was so mild as to be non-existent. There

was more sexual electricity in the one and only verbal exchange with George Chakiris.

Chakiris played a handsome, well-groomed Greek-Cypriot terrorist who was so fantastically patriotic that he even refused Turkish coffee. The soundtrack cued his every appearance, giving rise to false hopes that the star of *West Side Story* might at any moment start dancing.

Denholm Elliott, as an intelligence officer whose disguise was to pretend to be pissed out of his mind, was a U.S. cavalry of one, always arriving in the nick of time to save either the hero or the heroine.

Most critics felt that *The High Bright Sun* was a retrograde step in Bogarde's career and objected strongly to the way the tragedy of Cyprus was used merely as a pretty Mediterranean backdrop for a highly unlikely adventure yarn.

Dirk Bogarde in
The High Bright Sun.

BELOW
Dirk Bogarde and
Susan Strasberg in
The High Bright Sun.

Dirk Bogarde is undoubtedly one of the best screen actors working in Britain today.
ANN PACEY *Sun*

No actor on earth could make anything of a film as villey directed and scripted as *The High Bright Sun.*

ISABEL QUIGLY *Spectator*

Dirk Bogarde – who seems to get younger and smoother with every role he plays – does not put a foot wrong. Indeed, he conveys more with one half-raised eyebrow than most actors do with their entire anatomies.

MICHAEL THORNTON *Sunday Express*

Dirk Bogarde gives his usual smooth performance – rather tongue-in-cheek at times, and no wonder.

ERNEST BETTS *People*

DARLING 1965

directed by
John Schlesinger

OPPOSITE
Dirk Bogarde in
Darling.

BELOW
Dirk Bogarde and
Julie Christie in
Darling.

*D*arling, Britain's *La Dolce Vita*, was *the* swinging sixties film, a mordant satire on the shoddy-glossy world of advertising and fashion photography, a companion piece to *Nothing But The Best*, which charted the rise of a working-class *arriviste*.

John Schlesinger and the writer Frederick Raphael picked off their targets with caustic wit: the interview with the man-in-the-street giving his views on homosexuality, a spoof Pathé newsreel ('It isn't every day that a bride on her wedding day finds she is the mother of seven children'), an exhibition of an ex-convict's paintings, an upper-middle-class dinner-party, and the rich gorging themselves at an Oxfam fund-raising do.

The unendearing darling of the title was a selfish, superficial, ambitious, promiscuous model, a *poule de luxe*, climbing the social ladder, bed by bed, until she ends up an Italian princess, lonely but rich in a vast empty palace. Julie Christie, who played the destructive bitch in a performance which won her an 'Oscar', provided glitter and tawdriness in equal measure.

Bogarde played a television interviewer, frontman to a major arts programme, whose marriage darling breaks up, whose baby she aborts, whose faithfulness she so regularly fails to reciprocate, until finally when she comes crawling home, he pays her back in kind, in bed, before sending her packing to her husband.

There was one memorable scene when

he accuses her of being a tramp ('You're just a whore, baby, just a whore, and I don't take whores in taxis'). Bogarde has been asked to lose his temper in countless movies, but rarely has he lost it to better effect. The line was camp-theatrical, of course, but it did not come out of a melodramatic vacuum, as so often in the past, but out of all that had gone before and it was a perfect preparation for the scene immediately following on an escalator in the underground when darling really does behave like a whore.

Bogarde was so good that it came as a surprise to learn that not only was he not Schlesinger's first choice but that at one point he had very nearly been edited out of the film. The great strength of the performance (one of his finest) was that the man's decency was always totally believable, so much so that when darling got her richly deserved come-uppance, the scene was genuinely shocking because the action degraded him.

Bogarde won the British Film Academy's award for best actor.

Julie Christie and Dirk Bogarde in *Darling*.

But possibly the most notable achievement belongs to Dirk Bogarde, whose quiet agony turns the thankless part of the 'good guy' into a performance that outshines his portrayal as the furtive butler in *The Servant*, and makes a solid contribution to an already long list of famous British film characterisations. It is a memorable piece of acting, steeped in compassion and understanding, and worthy of Frederick Raphael's trenchant screenplay.

CLIVE HIRSCHHORN *Sunday Express*

And Dirk Bogarde's performance, in its quiet way, is one of the most powerfully effective of the year.

LEONARD MOSLEY *Daily Express*

And, of course, I don't have to say that Dirk Bogarde is absolutely superb as Robert. As a decent, worried man of conscience he is the only one you really care about. ANN PACEY *Sun*

Julie Christie and Dirk Bogarde in *Darling*.

Dirk Bogarde,
Monica Vitti and
Terence Stamp in
Modesty Blaise.

MODESTY BLAISE   1966

*My only interest in doing the film was to do a
kind of parody of the violence for violence's
sake of the spy and the Bond-type films.*

JOSEPH LOSEY

directed by
Joseph Losey

The serious intention got lost in
the making. *Modesty Blaise*, based
on Peter O'Donnell's *Evening
Standard* cartoon-strip, was all
style and no content: a 1960s mix of high
camp, pop-art and sick humour, out-
rageously costumed and set. The final
battle, with the Arabs driving out of the sea
in their mini-hydrofoils, was very *sheik* in a
frantic Mack Sennett sort of way.

20th Century Fox had wanted a female
companion for the James Bond films; what
they got was a modish, unfunny, highly
self-indulgent burlesque of sex and sadism,
seemingly aimed at interior decorators.
Modesty Blaise was as much designer
Richard Macdonald's film as Joseph
Losey's.

Monica Vitti in the title role was hardly
the terror of the underworld (more like a
refugee from Antonioni) though there was
one splendid moment when she dug her
nails into her side-kick Willie Garvin's back
and ripped off his skin to the audible agony
of the audience, until they discovered the
skin was false.

Bogarde was cast as the hyper-sensitive
arch-villain Gabriel, and very arch he was,
too, in his white wig and slit-eyed
spectacles, carrying a lilac parasol and
drinking from a long-stemmed goblet with
a goldfish swimming about in it. His retinue
included a clown, a kilted Scottish Presby-
terian accountant, a blond henchman
straight off the cover of a gay magazine,
and a lesbian executioner who strangles her

137

victims with her knees.

The one thing everybody remembers about his prissy performance (a performance he is on record as wishing to forget) is the image, surprisingly badly framed, of Gabriel staked out in the desert in the midday sun, gasping for *champagne* rather than water.

But the film really comes alive with the first appearance of Dirk Bogarde – the exquisite super-robber, hidden away in his op-art castle on a Mediterranean island, who can command a rocket interceptor but shrinks from the cries of boiling lobsters. Bogarde takes over the screen on every appearance.

Here is a cinema actor, becoming greater with every film, in obvious sympathy with an equally understanding director.

IAN WRIGHT *Guardian*

Dirk Bogarde is perhaps too essentially serious an actor to extract everything possible from Gabriel, the criminal fantasist with a mother complex. The scene in which he orders his rocket to shoot down an RAF plane, alternating tremolos of regret for the casualties with alarming exultation, ought to be either funnier or more abrasive, less or more true to some kind of life.

PENELOPE HOUSTON *Sight and Sound*

BELOW AND OPPOSITE
Dirk Bogarde in
Modesty Blaise.

ACCIDENT 1967

directed by
Joseph Losey

Three men — two rival Oxford dons (Bogarde and Stanley Baker) and a young undergraduate (Michael York) — all fall in love with an Austrian student (Jacqueline Sassard). The complexity of the relationships was drawn with the greatest subtlety and economy.

One of the highlights of the film was a desultory drunken conversation round the supper-table, the vicious malice wittily observed by author, director and actors. But, as usual, with a Harold Pinter script, the real dialogue was going on below the surface.

Bogarde's wistful, lonely, introverted philosophy tutor was one of his quietest performances, the frustration, guilt and self-loathing all having to be tactfully suggested rather than stated or shown. There was always the feeling, unwarranted perhaps, that the tutor might also be in love with the undergraduate.

The off-screen accident, and the sound of screeching brakes and tortured metal, which opened and closed the film, were a perfect audible complement for the invisible scars and silent weeping which was going on inside the character.

One of Bogarde's most difficult scenes (which he carried off with great success) was when he returned home unexpectedly to find his rival had been to bed with the girl, and he had to sustain and contain his anger over a very long period without the help of any dialogue. His muted, yet blazing rage was visible only in the making of an omelette.

Joseph Losey directed Bogarde in an imaginative flashback with a former mistress (Delphine Seyrig) in which the

Jacqueline Sassard
and Dirk Bogarde in
Accident.

Joseph Losey, Vivien Merchant and Dirk Bogarde on the set of *Accident*.
OPPOSITE
Dirk Bogarde and Michael York in *Accident*.

fractured dialogue was out of synch with the frame, giving the deliberate banality of the lines a resonance they most certainly would not have had if the sequence had been played straight.

The only scene which misfired (so badly it should have been cut) was, ironically, the one in which Harold Pinter himself ap-

peared, going wildly over the top as a bullish television producer, in a jarring parody of Pinter.

Bogarde has described *Accident* as his *Hamlet*, his most important and satisfying role, because it is the only one of all his performances in which he finds absolutely nothing of himself.

Dirk Bogarde,
Vivien Merchant and
Michael York in
Accident.

OPPOSITE
Jacqueline Sassard,
Dirk Bogarde and
Stanley Baker in
Accident.

I have only praise for the rest of the performers – especially Dirk Bogarde, who is incapable, these days, of anything less than brilliance. Though the character is basically weak – it is a weakness which dominates the screen.

CLIVE HIRSCHHORN *Sunday Express*

It's also, in my opinion, the best film Dirk Bogarde has ever made.

ERNEST BETTS *People*

With his usual quiet perceptiveness, Bogarde holds the whole film together.

FELIX BARKER *Evening News*

As a philosophy-don husband, Dirk Bogarde is just about perfect: he acts like a man who's had a spinal tap. He's a virtuoso at this civilised, stifled anguish racket, better even than Ralph Richardson used to be at suppressed emotion because he is so much more ambiguous that we can't be sure what he's suppressing. He aches all the time all over, like an all-purpose sufferer for a television commercial – locked in, with a claustrophobia of his own body and sensibility. Bogarde looks rather marvellous going through his middle-age frustration routines.

PAULINE KAEL *New Yorker*

Our Mother's House, a disturbing modern Gothic tale, was billed as 'the children's story that is not for children' – though for those who knew Julian Gloag's novel and Jack Clayton's earlier work and were hoping for a marriage of *The Turn of the Screw* and *Lord of the Flies*, the film was perhaps not disturbing enough.

The setting was a crumbling Victorian house in a London suburb. Seven children, their ages ranging from thirteen to four, fearing they will be sent to an orphanage if their mother's death becomes known, bury her in the back garden, build a tabernacle to her in the potting shed, and tell everybody she is in hospital. The performances Jack Clayton drew from the children, especially Pamela Franklin and Mark Lester, were quite remarkable.

Our Mother's House, macabre and sentimental, failed at the box office, having been given no help by the critics, who concentrated on its flaws of improbability rather than its strengths of atmospheric detail. Its rehabilitation is long over-due.

Bogarde was cast as the long-lost father, a cockney ne'er-do-well, who comes home to see what's in it for him, filling the house with booze and women and living off his

directed by
Jack Clayton

Dirk Bogarde in
Our Mother's House.

OPPOSITE
Louis
Sheldon-Williams,
Dirk Bogarde,
Gustav Henry and
Pamela Franklin in
Our Mother's House.

OPPOSITE
Sarah Nicholls,
Pamela Franklin,
Dirk Bogarde, Louis
Sheldon-Williams,
Parnham Wallace,
Margaret Brooks,
John Gugolka,
Gustav Henry and
Mark Lester in
Our Mother's House.

Dirk Bogarde in
Our Mother's House.

wife's post-office savings. When the money runs out he decides to sell the house and put them all in an orphanage.

His big dramatic scene came when he tells them that their sainted mother was a whore and that they are all bastards by different fathers and that not one of them is his. The scene ended in his brutal murder at the poker-held hands of the young girl (Pamela Franklin) who had loved him most.

Bogarde was quoted in the French film magazine *Ecran* as saying that he adores children. ('They are excellent actors. When one works with them it is as if one is working with the great film stars.') His pleasure was so obvious that when the volte-face came, highly impressive though he was, the sheer viciousness the scene revealed seemed to belong to quite a different person.

Dirk Bogarde traces the rascally but not insensitive Charlie's shifts between bewilderment, ingratiation and exasperated rage, with that immaculate precision and velvety strength which we have come to expect of him.

RAYMOND DURGNAT *Films and Filming*

Dirk Bogarde's performance does not really illuminate the character – or perhaps he simply felt defeated by the script and retreated into his present interpretation: a formulization, abstracted from any sort of real life, of a cheery, cheeky, character comic, in which, with transparent circulation, sinister undercurrents are allowed gradually to surface.

DAVID ROBINSON *Financial Times*

Dirk Bogarde as the husband is efficient as always, but completely miscast to my mind.   PATRICK GIBBS *Sunday Telegraph*

Mr Bogarde is now surely one of the best actors of our time.

HOLLIS ALPERT *Saturday Review*

Charlie Hook is an impossibly under-developed and poorly written shadow of a part. Bogarde, looking like an ageing Cliff Richard, does the best he can with him, but the performance is never convincing.

CLIVE HIRSCHHORN *Sunday Express*

SEBASTIAN 1968

**directed by
David Greene**

*S*ebastian, a romantic spy-thriller, is not, of course, to be confused with Derek Jarman's homo-erotic movie of the same name. This Sebastian was no saint fending off gay Latin-speaking soldiers, but an Oxford don, a master code-breaker, surrounded by hordes of bright girls (not a man in sight) who takes his manual to bed, even when he is on the job, and is so brilliant he can decypher the code in a baby's rattle.

The film was, to quote Bogarde, a paralysing non-event. The screenplay had no idea what it was doing and did it badly in such a variety of styles and unrelated levels as to be largely incomprehensible.

Sebastian began on a flippant note and with so much padding that it seemed as if the story would never begin. Once it did begin, it should have concentrated on the code-breaking; instead it preferred to concentrate on the highly unlikely affair (Saturdays only) with a kookie girl and an equally unlikely affair with a member of staff who gets pregnant. Susannah York behaved as if she were in a screwball comedy of the 1930s, while Bogarde, looking like 'a poor lost lamb', behaved as if

Ronald Fraser and
Dirk Bogarde in
Sebastian.

he were in something a bit more serious. The two roles never gelled.

John Gielgud played the head of intelligence and Nigel Davenport played his number two with such obvious unpleasantness that it was slightly disappointing to find that they were not, as is normal in spy films and real life, working for the other side. The real villain was a brutal pimp, played by Ronald Fraser, and there was an extraordinary and totally unexplained sequence (trendily photographed) in which Bogarde is drugged up to the eyeballs, kidnapped and nearly persuaded to jump from the roof of a high-rise building.

Bogarde was at his best in a tiny scene telling the head of intelligence's hatchet men exactly what he thinks of them.

Dirk Bogarde, as usual, is invaluable.

PENELOPE HOUSTON *Spectator*

Bogarde somehow manages to remain his charming self throughout and for that, and that alone, I congratulate him.

ANN PACEY *Sun*

In the title role, Bogarde provides added proof that he is a fine film actor with an extraordinary range of sensibilities.

Time Magazine

There is a plot, of course, but it is never allowed to get in the way of the fun or the brilliance of the dialogue and the acting. From Dirk Bogarde one has come to expect nothing less.

RICHARD ROUD *Guardian*

THE FIXER   1969

directed by
John Frankenheimer

*T*he Fixer, a ponderous, interminable diatribe against injustice, concentrated on the brutality rather than the spiritual progress of the prisoner (a subject for the French director Robert Bresson, perhaps), piling on the agony to such a harrowing degree that the film became as much an endurance test for the audience as for the fixer, Yakov Bok.

Bok (Alan Bates) was a Russian peasant, a Jew, living in the Ukraine in 1911, who was falsely accused of the ritual murder of a Christian boy and subjected, for political reasons, to every mental and physical torture to force him to confess; but Bok did not break, rejecting a phoney pardon and insisting on a trial. He was ultimately acquitted. In its day, the case was an international *cause célèbre* to rival Dreyfus.

Bogarde was cast in the small but important role of the compassionate government lawyer Bibikov, who believes in Bok's innocence and helps him to understand that a confession will condemn not only him but the whole Jewish race as well.

In Bernard Malamud's novel, Bibikov was a bourgeois; the film turned him into a pince-nezed, melancholy, prim aristocrat, a member of a doomed class soon to be swept away. He was last seen hanging from a beam in a cell in the prison, having been murdered by the Tsarist authorities.

There was nothing for me to do. Invariably when I have too little to do, I always do too much, being under the impression that I have to do something to justify my salary.

DIRK BOGARDE quoted by
ALAIN GAREL *Ecran*

There is yet another splendid characterisation from Dirk Bogarde, surely one of the very best British actors we have, as Bibikov, the lawyer.

CLIVE HIRSCHHORN *Sunday Express*

Dirk Bogarde turns in a beautifully precise performance as the lawyer who befriends the persecuted man.

IAN CHRISTIE *Daily Express*

It is becoming almost a critical cliché to praise Mr Bogarde as the saviour of films. Here again Mr Bogarde displays his habitual level-eyed authority as a lawyer of integrity – perhaps even cheats a bit by implying enigmatic depths in his relationship with the prisoner. When he meets an untimely end the film's reins slacken leaving us with no catharsis.

DEREK PROUSE *Sunday Times*

Dirk Bogarde – who nowadays saves as many pictures as he appears in – gives his usual exquisite performance.

PENELOPE MORTIMER *Observer*

Dirk Bogarde is, as always, ostentatiously sensitive.   WILFRID SHEED *Esquire*

Dirk Bogarde in *The Fixer*.

152

JUSTINE 1969

directed by
George Cukor

Hollywood's decadent, fabled Alexandria had all the mystery, allure and sin of Derry and Tom's roof garden.

DIRK BOGARDE *Snakes and Ladders*

Justine attempted the impossible: to condense and film the unfilmable *Alexandria Quartet*. The project (eight years in the making, two directors and five writers) was doomed from the start.

Lawrence Durrell hoped that *Justine* would not turn his novel into 'a sort of *Peyton Place* with camels'. But take away the elaborate literary structure and the jewelled prose and all you are left with is lust, murder, gun-running, child-prostitutes, political intrigue, homosexuality, treachery, male transvestism, incest and Coptic Christians. Of course, this may be more than enough for most cinemagoers; only the *cognoscenti*, after all, are going to miss the glass-eyed pederast and the one-handed lesbian.

However, no studio-bound picture is ever going to be able to do justice to Alexandria in all its decadence, corruption and perversion. *Justine* without Alexandria is like *Hamlet* without the prince. A few interpolated snapshots of tourist Egypt will hardly suffice; and even less so when the colour changes alarmingly from shot to shot. The street scenes looked as if they had been filmed in the sets for *Casablanca*.

Anouk Aimée was splendid as the enigmatic Justine, a beautiful and dangerous

Cliff Gorman,
Dirk Bogarde,
John Vernon,
Anouk Aimée and
Michael York in
Justine.

nymphomaniac and conspirator. Bogarde was cast as the British Consul, Pursewarden, who refuses to walk through her sexual turnstile. 'When are you going to stop being a sin-cushion into which we have to stick our rusty pins?' he asks. (It was said that not a day passed on which Pursewarden failed to delight everybody with his savage wit.)

Bogarde was not the Pursewarden of the novel (strongly built, small moustache and seedy) and for a long time he didn't seem to be in the film, having little to do except smirk on the periphery and be ever-so-slightly camp. His self-disgust was established by spitting his drink at his reflection in the mirror. His most arresting scene was the one in which he learns that the English ambassador is going to marry his sister and is totally at a loss for words. The audience was equally totally at a loss to know why; and it wasn't until much later in the film that they learned he had been having an affair with his sister.

I am particularly happy about their choice of Dirk Bogarde; in his performances there is always a kind of deep introspective and rather sorrowing quality — even when he is playing comedy. He suggests that most of his life, like that of an artist, is lived below the surface.

LAWRENCE DURRELL

The usually competent Dirk Bogarde appears to be worrying about why he ever allowed himself to appear in the picture. He has so little to do that when he finally bites down his capsule we can only wonder why he didn't apply for a different assignment.

HOLLIS ALPERT *Saturday Review*

Dirk Bogarde in *Justine*.

But the real performance of the film, as happens these days with almost tiresome regularity, comes from Dirk Bogarde as Pursewarden. While he is on the screen the whole thing lights up; from the rather skimpy material he is given he constructs a really complex, satisfying, contradictory character.

JOHN RUSSELL TAYLOR *The Times*

Bogarde sails through the muddles with an air of tired professionalism that suits the part admirably. The others seem merely tired. ANN PACEY *Sun*

But really only Bogarde rises above the inanities. As Pursewarden, he manages to create a genuinely tormented figure and to deliver his lines as though they were worth the trouble. TOM MILNE *Observer*

OH! WHAT A LOVELY WAR   1969

directed by
Richard
Attenborough

Bogarde was one of many stars who rallied round, accepting cameo parts so that Richard Attenborough could have the box-office names he needed to make *Oh! What A Lovely War* commercially viable.

The roll call included John Gielgud, Jack Hawkins, Ian Holm, John Mills, Kenneth More, Laurence Olivier, Michael Redgrave, Vanessa Redgrave, Ralph Richardson, Maggie Smith and Susannah York.

The satire on the officer class and the terrible carnage of the First World War no longer had the impact it had had in Joan Littlewood's memorable production at the Theatre Royal, Stratford, in the East End of London. The very theatricality, the studied artificiality of the idiom and construction, which had been so effective on the stage, just did not work when transferred to Brighton Pier and acted out on the screen.

Bogarde and Susannah York were seen briefly as the idle, thoughtless rich, discussing the terrible privations of their war over a glass of champagne. The Bogarde character determines to make the supreme sacrifice — he will not drink any German wines from his cellar for the duration.

Dirk Bogarde in
*Oh! What A Lovely
War.*

I am making this film for the younger generation who do not know what Nazism was like. They must know from this.

LUCHINO VISCONTI

directed by
Luchino Visconti
English title:
The Damned

The Damned, an allegory of Nazi Germany, described the fall of a great and powerful munitions family, their political and sexual corruption complementing the perversion and moral decay of the Third Reich. There were many who thought the story a load of old Krupp.

Visconti had wanted to call his film *Götterdämmerung*, and certainly it played like some enormous Grand Opera with a highly coloured and ludicrous libretto which few could either follow or take seriously. The dubbing only made the film more operatic.

The baroque excesses were such as to make the Houses of Atreus and Usher look like mere amateurs. There was, on the last count, patricide, matricide, incest, madness, homosexuality, pederasty, transvestism, sado-masochism, plus an orgy or two, a general massacre and a bit of arson on the side.

The Damned, a flamboyantly camp-theatrical reconstruction of the period (the decor, clothes, hair styles and costumes being far more interesting than the script) was notable for four set-pieces. First, the funeral procession through the factory site; second, a protracted homosexual orgy (boys in black lace panties, that sort of thing); third, the night of the long knives when Rhoem's Brown Shirts were massacred by the rival SS (lots of naked bodies *in flagrante delicto*, splashed with red paint); and fourth, a mock-wedding ceremony in

Dirk Bogarde in *The Damned*.

157

Ingrid Thulin and
Dirk Bogarde in
The Damned.

which the unhappy pair, having signed the register, retire to the next room, forced to commit suicide.

Bogarde was cast as Bruckmann, the outsider murdering his way to the top of the firm. Visconti had offered the part to Bogarde because he had been impressed by the cynicism and geniality he had brought to the role of Charlie Hook in *Our Mother's House*. Bogarde, not liking the script, turned him down three times and would have been well advised to turn him down a fourth, being totally miscast. His very English performance, neither cynical nor genial, more bourgeois than Borgia, was torn to shreds, first by the editor and then by the critics. He was meant to be playing a Macbeth-like figure to Ingrid Thulin's glacially Ayrian Lady Macbeth; but the part was so incomplete that the impotent screaming at the dinner-table – his big scene – coming as it did out of absolutely nothing, was meaningless.

Helmut Berger's high-pitched debut as drag-artist, pederast and mother-raper was in keeping with Visconti's self-indulgent upholstered vulgarity. The best performance, however, was by Helmut Griem who played a murderous Nazi without any visible kinks.

I was bloody good in it, though you'd never know that in England. In England it must have seemed like the first time an actor with his name above the title had played his entire role with his back to the camera.

DIRK BOGARDE quoted by
BARRY NORMAN *The Times*

I was disappointed in Dirk Bogarde because I can no longer think of him being as less than brilliant.

PENELOPE MORTIMER *Observer*

MORTE A VENEZIA 1971

directed by
Luchino Visconti
English title:
Death in Venice

To be asked by Visconti to play in Death in Venice *is like Larry Olivier inviting you to play Hamlet. Only better, much better.*

DIRK BOGARDE
quoted by MARGARET HINXMAN
Sunday Telegraph

Thomas Mann's *Death in Venice* became, in Visconti's hands, a funeral elegy not just for lost youth but also for a vanished and opulent Edwardian world. The film took its time: a beautiful, melancholy, measured 128 minutes in which so much was said without words that the screenplay would have been better for the excision of what dialogue there was, especially in all those unnecessary flashbacks.

The period detail and social nuance were lovingly re-created and meticulously observed, the camera roaming round eavesdropping on the rich holidaying at the Hôtel des Bains. Visconti was as much a voyeur as Aschenbach. The *mise-en-scène* was superb.

The film unequivocally identified Aschenbach with Gustav Mahler (rather than Mann) and used his Third and Fifth Symphonies to lush-romantic effect – wave upon wave of emotion – which was totally at variance with Aschenbach's intellectual and virginal rigidity.

The girlishly beautiful Tadzio, with his golden hair and slim body, was as androgynous as any Italian classical sculptor could desire: an Angel of Death who was a real flirt, *un garçon fatal*, well aware of what was going on. Bjorn Andresen, the young Swedish actor, in his pretty sailor-suit and swim-suit, constantly looking over his shoulder with a come-hither look, gave Aschenbach such palpitations of the heart ('You must never smile like that at anyone . . . I love you') that death, the final orgasm, was as much the result of lust as cholera and old age.

The fourteen-year-old boy is meant to symbolize all that is unattainable – spiritual beauty, perfection in life and art, lost youth. Mann's novella is not really about homosexual love; or, to put it another way, the unattainable Tadzio, in Visconti's film, seemed all too readily available, a gay Adonis in the making.

Bogarde immediately established the composer's vulnerability in the presence of death in the slow journey across the lagoon with a Charon-like gondolier. He captured perfectly the fastidiousness, the vanity, the little outbursts of temper; his obsession with the boy was always as absurd as it was abject.

The final degradation at the barber's was grotesque: the dye, paint, powder, far from giving him back his youth, merely made him look like the obscene old quean he had met on the boat when he first arrived in Venice. The scene which followed, in the rat-ridden piazza, when Aschenbach is caught in the storm and sinks feverishly to the ground by the fountain, the dye, paint, powder running down his face, staining his immaculate white suit, was opera without the singing.

But Bogarde's largely wordless performance was notable as much for its wit as for its pathos. Two moments stood out in particular: his bemused and ever-so-slightly shocked reaction to the boys kissing on the beach, and the *frisson* he got from his close proximity to the young lads in the small, rickety lift in the Hôtel des Bains.

Dirk Bogarde in
Death in Venice.

OVERLEAF
Dirk Bogarde and
Bjorn Andresen in
Death in Venice.

160

I've long admired Bogarde as a superb actor. But never have I had more cause for delight in an actor's skill and nerve than watching him in this role which will surely be the very capstone of his career.

ALEXANDER WALKER *Evening Standard*

Bogarde gives his most powerful and moving performance. This is great acting.

MADELEINE HORMSWORTH *Sunday Mirror*

In shoes that seemed to be filled with glass marbles, he hobbles about Venice, leching the boy, and giving a very good impersonation of a middle-aged actor playing a very old actor.

FERGUS CASHIN *Sun*

For some reason there is still a tendency to treat this remarkably good actor rather patronisingly, to appear slightly surprised that he can act at all. Perhaps this dates from his early days with Rank, but after his performance here I trust all doubts will be exorcised. It's a truly great performance in that every irritable word and old-maidish gesture adds to our knowledge of what goes on inside his head. If he doesn't win an Oscar, there's no justice.

GEORGE MELLY *Observer*

The more I think about it, the more it begins to look like a masterpiece.

CHRISTOPHER HUDSON *Spectator*

Luchino Visconti and Dirk Bogarde on the set of *Death in Venice*.

Dirk Bogarde as the tortured composer gives a performance that is both sensitive and compelling. It is his fine acting that saves the film from overall tedium.

DAVID GILLARD *Daily Sketch*

There can be no doubt that Dirk Bogarde has given here the performance of his life, confirming his pre-eminence among screen actors: a portrayal of infinite detail which never lets the external cleverness of gesture, stance and make-up obscure the character deeply rooted underneath.

MARGARET HINXMAN *Sunday Telegraph*

ABOVE AND LEFT
Dirk Bogarde in
Death in Venice.

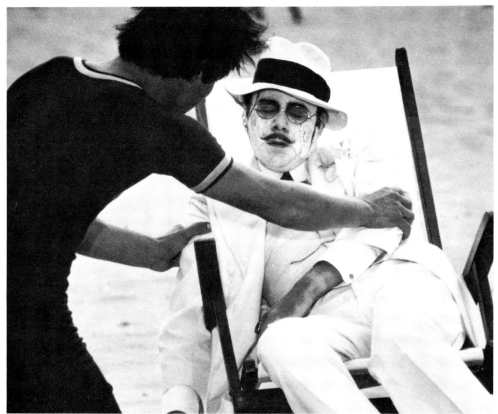

THE SERPENT 1974

directed by
Henri Verneuil
U.S. title: *Night
Flight From Moscow*

The *Serpent* was based on the famous spy scandals of the 1950s, updated to the 1970s, and starred Henry Fonda as head of CIA, Bogarde as head of MI6 and Yul Brynner as a high-ranking KGB officer, defecting to the West with a long list of European traitors, who are killed off and then all found to have been clean men.

The film, a multi-lingual, French-German-Italian production, adopted a quasi-documentary approach, giving pride of place to the elaborate electronic equipment at CIA headquarters, and still managed to make fact look like fiction.

Bogarde, smooth and cynical, was the rotten apple in the Homburg hat who had been working for the Russians for thirty years. It was a Kim Philby sort of role which he acted in a heavy-handed and somewhat camp 'old dear' manner, as if he were auditioning for Burgess: 'Don't use words like traitor to me. I have been a Marxist since I was nineteen.' His best scenes were the ones he shared with Philippe Noiret, playing his French opposite number.

Dirk Bogarde plays Boyle. It's a role which calls for no more animation than a tailor's dummy. ARTHUR THIRKELL *Daily Mirror*

Bogarde's first appearance, in background and reaction shots, are in his fractionally-raised eyebrow style, which augurs not well, and, indeed, he droops urbanely through his scenes, shifting inside his suit, rolling his tongue from cheek to cheek — offering, in short, all the shrugs, pouts and minute disclaimers that usually indicate he has been given nothing to occupy his mind. RUSSELL DAVIES *Observer*

Dirk Bogarde is a most unlikely dedicated Marxist. VIRGINIA DIGNAM *Morning Star*

Dirk Bogarde and Henry Fonda in
The Serpent.

IL PORTIERE DI NOTTE 1974

**directed by
Liliana Cavani
English title:
*The Night Porter***

OPPOSITE
Charlotte Rampling
and Dirk Bogarde in
The Night Porter.

BELOW
Dirk Bogarde in
The Night Porter.

The Night Porter wasn't pornography for the dirty mac brigade; but then equally it wasn't, as the *Daily Mirror* warned its readers, exactly family entertainment.

The film divided the critics and the public, nobody quite certain whether they were watching a boring work of art or a boring advertisement for sado-masochism.

Bogarde played the title role, one of a group of ex-Nazis who protect themselves by eliminating witnesses who might bring them to trial. They were all Grosz caricatures, the cartoon element emphasised by the over-loud dubbing which made what they were saying seem to be coming out of large bubbles above their heads rather than out of their mouths.

Liliana Cavani's screenplay described an affair between a night porter of a Viennese hotel and an internationally famous conductor's wife, intercut with scenes from their previous affair, some fifteen years earlier in a concentration camp, where she was an inmate and he, a young SS officer.

In the camp, and it was very camp, there was a topless Charlotte Rampling whose braces-and-trousers cabaret act was rewarded with the decapitated head of a prisoner who had tormented her. There was also licking of wounds and taking of photographs. Meanwhile back in Vienna, there was broken glass to walk on, fingers to suck, chains to be tied to, and a scene which was to do for the jam trade what *Last Tango in Paris* had done already for the butter trade. There were moments, especially when the couple were starving it out in a garret, when the two actors came very near to corpsing at the absurdity of the perversity they were being asked to enact.

British distributors, like their American counterparts, had no idea what to do with the film and at one point it looked, despite its success in Paris, as if it would never be released in England. In desperation Bogarde took matters into his own hands and arranged a private viewing for four critics who had consistently influenced and encouraged his career. They were Dilys Powell, Margaret Hinxman, Felix Barker and Alexander Walker. Dilys Powell found the film brilliant.

Charlotte Rampling and Dirk Bogarde in *The Night Porter*.

And did you know that the preview of Night Porter *in the States was held in a theatre lined with black leather, and the critics sat in black leather seats with chains across them, and there were match-hooks with whips on them? The only way they knew how to sell it was pornography.*

DIRK BOGARDE quoted by
DAVID ROBINSON *The Times*

It is one of the most powerful films I have seen in years. It contains the best performance Dirk Bogarde has ever given.
MARGARET HINXMAN *Sunday Telegraph*

The answer is that despite flaws it has an extraordinary quality, terrifying but compulsive. Oh yes, it's difficult all right – but it's a difficulty our film people should regard as a challenge not an excuse for ignoring. FELIX BARKER *Evening News*

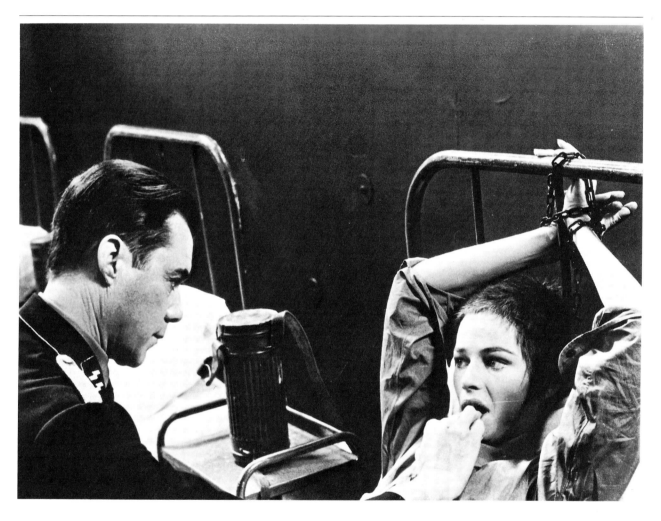

It just breeds disgust.

ALEXANDER WALKER *Evening Standard*

I might have found the film degrading if I had not found most of its plodding, portentous footage both ludicrous and risible.　　　PHILIP FRENCH *The Times*

Dirk Bogarde is magnificent as the guilt-ridden ex-Nazi whose entire life is lived at one remove from reality.

VIRGINIA DIGNAM *Morning Star*

After such pictures as *Victim, The Servant, Darling, Modesty Blaise, Accident, The Damned, Justine, Death in Venice*, he is just over-qualified for Max – he's also over-exposed. We know his neurasthenic tricks – the semaphoric eyebrows, the twitching mouth, the sneak vindictive gleam, the pinch of suffering. His warmed-over performance here has all the surprise of the *Cesar Frank Symphony in D minor*.

PAULINE KAEL *New Yorker*

Dirk Bogarde and Charlotte Rampling in *The Night Porter*.

PERMISSION TO KILL   1975

directed by
Cyril Frankel

Frederic Forrest and
Dirk Bogarde in
Permission to Kill.

Permission to Kill was a preposterous and largely incomprehensible espionage thriller in which Bogarde was cast as a ruthless British intelligence officer with orders to stop a political exile returning home to save his country from fascism.

The character was a very smooth and efficient manipulator, so immersed in a daily round of bribery, blackmail and murder he no longer knows what truth is. Truth is what he makes it. Bogarde caught the chilling nastiness perfectly, even managing to give the dialogue (which defeated everybody else) a certain authority. There was a short conversation on the phone with his wife to establish that underneath the cold-blooded façade he was actually a nice, normal family man. This was a lot of nonsense and should have been cut. Underneath it all, he was totally evil; and, according to another spy, gay with it, an accusation which was repeated with monotonous regularity by Timothy Dalton every time he appeared, though the idea was never developed nor denied.

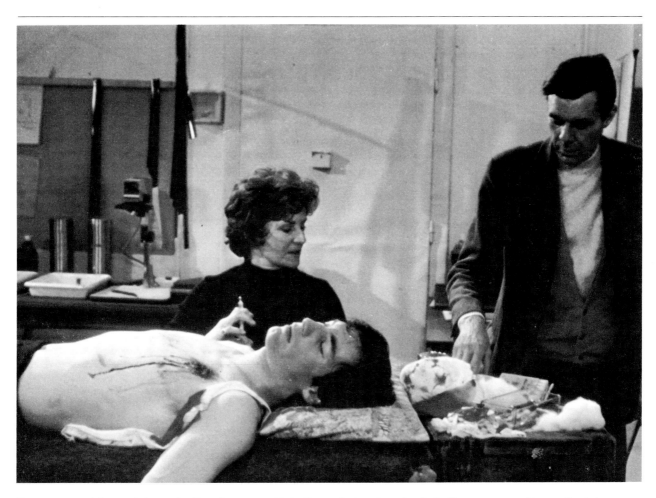

It got me out of that awful rut after Death in Venice *and* Night Porter *when most of the scripts I was offered featured ageing queers and perverts.*

DIRK BOGARDE quoted by
MARGARET HINXMAN *Daily Mail*

The acting is uniformly stilted, not excepting Dirk Bogarde, who occasionally gives a twitch of his cheek to show that he has a mordant sense of humour, and a twitch at the corner of his mouth to indicate buried moral scruples.

PHILIP FRENCH *The Times*

Only Bogarde, in a hopelessly half-developed part, says his lines with any conviction. They scarcely deserve the compliment he thereby pays them.

DEREK MALCOLM *Guardian*

If I had not seen him before I should be asking who he was, what he had done, where he comes from. I know what he has done. But he submerges himself so completely in the film that one can forget. One can simply watch an actor not indeed new, but repeatedly transformed.

DILYS POWELL *Sunday Times*

Peggy Sinclair, Timothy Dalton and Dirk Bogarde in *Permission to Kill.*

PROVIDENCE 1977

directed by
Alain Resnais

For nearly fourteen years Alain Resnais and Bogarde had wanted to make a film together. When they finally came to make *Providence*, Resnais' first film in English, a major work with a brilliant, complex and witty script by David Mercer, Bogarde was disconcerted to find that he was not playing, as he had thought he would be, the leading role.

Providence, a characteristic bit of legerdemain and perhaps Resnais' best film since *L'Année Dernière à Marienbad*, was in fact about a 78-year-old dying author (John Gielgud in his finest screen role) spending his last night plotting his latest novel while drinking chilled chablis and sticking pesaries up his backside. The author tries out various permutations, using his family to flesh out his undeveloped characters. The creative process was constantly being interrupted by memories and nightmares until it was impossible to know what was real and what was fantasy, so often was the line of demarcation blurred.

Bogarde played the novelist's elder married son. He appeared in his father's novel as a cold and priggish lawyer, cynical, sarcastic and boiling with jealousy. The waspish wit could hardly have been more theatrical; it out-Webbed Clifton Webb. Some people, rather strangely, accused Bogarde of being camp as if the petrified character his father so maliciously and humiliatingly had invented for him was not meant to be camp. The real son — sensitive, unassuming, kind and obviously hurt by his father's rejection — did not appear until the very end of the film; and when he did, the contrast, beautifully judged by Bogarde, was one of the chief surprises and pleasures of the film.

Dirk Bogarde and
Ellen Burstyn in
Providence.

174

Dirk Bogarde and
Elaine Stritch in
Providence.

OPPOSITE
David Warner,
Ellen Burstyn,
John Gielgud and
Dirk Bogarde in
Providence.

And Dirk Bogarde's barrister, limp-wristed
and reptilian, is the most venomously
witty performance this ever-improving
actor has given.

NIGEL ANDREWS *Financial Times*

Dirk Bogarde, as the author's elder son, a
lawyer, affects mannerisms more fitting to
a peevish fashion designer than a
courtroom prosecutor.

JUDITH SIMONS *Daily Express*

Who can distinguish between Dirk
Bogarde acting arch and just acting as
usual?   PAULINE KAEL *New Yorker*

Dirk Bogarde as the son, Claud, is all brisk,
crackle and pop, dry as toast and twice as
brittle, like a middle-aged juvenile in a
weekly rep rehearsal of a lesser Noël
Coward.   ALAN BRIEN *Sunday Times*

Gielgud is the dominant voice, but in any
other context Bogarde's transition from
repulsively chill lawyer, as 'written' by his
father, to real-life hesitancy of an adoring,
too-upright son would be rated a *tour de
force*.

TOM HUTCHINSON *Sunday Telegraph*

A BRIDGE TOO FAR   1977

directed by
Richard
Attenborough

A Bridge Too Far, the epic documentary about the Battle of Arnhem in World War Two, had so many famous faces in cameo roles that it came to be known as 'A Star Too Many'.

When it was announced that Bogarde had accepted the role of Sir Frederick 'Boy' Browning, the general who commanded the airborne troops (and would be later depicted as ignoring vital reconnaissance information about the build-up of German tanks), Browning's widow, Daphne du Maurier, was not pleased, feeling he was completely wrong. Talking about her husband to the *Daily Express*, she was quoted as saying: 'He was an elegant and fastidious man but never effete.' She could not have taken much comfort from Attenborough's words, also quoted in the same article: 'If General Browning rode into battle wearing pearl-grey gloves that's the way we shall show him.'

When the film was released General Sir John Hackett, military adviser to the film, wrote to *The Times*, complaining that the portrayal of Browning as a superficial, heartless and flippant officer was untruthful and unkind, wounding and offensive: 'The portrayal of Boy Browning is the outstanding blot in an otherwise generally fair picture.'

Bogarde's laconic performance predictably also outraged Miss du Maurier, who was quoted in the *Daily Express* as saying, 'My God they wouldn't have dared do this if "Boy" had been still alive. He would have roasted them.'

It was Bogarde's final scene which gave most offence, the one in which Major General Robert Urquhart (Sean Connery)

reports that of the sixteen thousand men who had gone into battle, fewer than two thousand had returned. Browning's only response is to say that 'Monty was very proud of them'.

The chief, least justified simplification, resides in making General Browning bear the brunt of the responsibility for the operation's failure, a decision reinforced by a twitchily neurotic performance by Dirk Bogarde at his most uningratiating.

PHILIP FRENCH *Observer*

As portrayed by Dirk Bogarde and, of course, by the script-writer, who is William Goldman, this general is not one I would have trusted to run a cocktail party.

PATRICK GIBBS *Daily Telegraph*

It is not so much *what* Bogarde says as the way he says it. In short, Bogarde interpreted the role badly, playing it — according to one of the film's military advisers — 'like a captain in the Pay Corps'.

PETER DUNN *Sunday Times*

Both Richard Attenborough and Sir John Hackett felt obliged to answer this last criticism, Attenborough taking full responsibility for the portrayal, and Hackett apologising for his unguarded, off-the-cuff remarks about the Pay Corps, which he had not thought were going to be repeated.

Sean Connery and Dirk Bogarde in
A Bridge Too Far.

DESPAIR 1978

directed by Rainer
Werner Fassbinder

*D*espair, the prolific Fassbinder's first film in English, dedicated to Artaud, Van Gogh and Zurn, was a stylish and stylized mixture of psychological thriller, existential angst and grotesque marital comedy, set in George Grosz's Berlin in the early 1930s on the eve of the Third Reich. Much of the story was photographed through Art Deco glass, giving the plot an additional sophisticated obscurity.

Bogarde played Hermann, a schizophrenic chocolate manufacturer, a Russian émigré, with an acute identity crisis and a Dostoyevsky-like obsession with murder, who is married to a stupid and blatantly faithless wife, a fleshy, feather-brained cockatoo, wittily acted by Andrea Ferreol, who was more often than not in the nude. 'Intelligence', he tells her, 'would take the bloom off your carnality.' He enjoys nothing better than standing outside himself observing himself making love to her.

When Hermann meets a tramp he believes to be his double, he kills him and takes on his identity. The irony is that the tramp looks nothing like him and he is arrested practically immediately. The actual moment of arrest ('I'm a film actor ... I'm coming out ... Don't look at the camera ... I'm coming out') paid homage to both the Hollywood gangster movie and Norma Desmond's exit in *Sunset Boulevard*.

In his autobiography, *An Orderly Man*, Bogarde says his performance in *Despair* is the best screen performance he has ever given; and certainly the final stages of the crack-up, following the murder, when he is on the run, were very impressive with their powerful close-ups of his deeply anguished face.

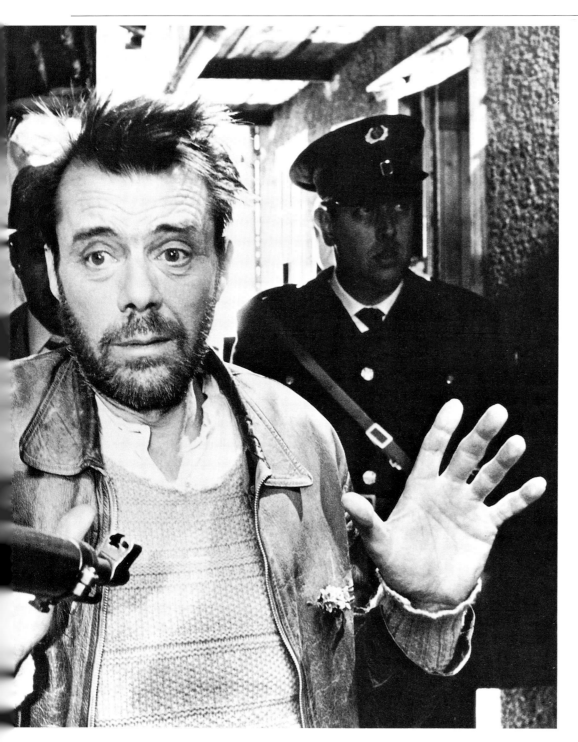

Dirk Bogarde in
Despair.

Volger Spengler,
Dirk Bogarde and
Andrea Ferreol in
Despair.

OPPOSITE
Dirk Bogarde in
Despair.

If the film is a triumph – and in its
idiosyncratic fashion, I think it is – it is
primarily Bogarde's triumph. He has
always been a courageous actor. Here, all
his qualities of finesse and subtlety coupled
with ruthless insight, cohere in a portrait of
extraordinary power.
MARGARET HINXMAN *Daily Mail*

Bogarde, an actor on intimate terms with
movie cameras, manages to give an always
watchable presence to a character who has
no real existence in human terms.
ALAN BRIEN *Sunday Times*

Bogarde gives his usual staunch
performance in a rotten role.
JOHN COLEMAN *New Statesman*

Fassbinder is also unable to control
Bogarde who is allowed to wander all over
the film, undisciplined and therefore
diminished. Bogarde is too fond of his
eyebrow raising, eye flashing and looks of
arrogant amusement to be allowed to go
undirected.
NICHOLAS WAPSHOTT *Scotsman*

Dirk Bogarde catches the fastidious
detached aspect of the character, but
signals the inner stress a little too
powerfully through that now famous
twitch and that familiar lip-fingering
motion.   PHILIP FRENCH *Observer*

MAY WE BORROW YOUR HUSBAND? 1986

directed by
Bob Mahoney

David Yelland,
Francis Matthews
and Dirk Bogarde in
*May We Borrow Your
Husband?*

*It was in the end a comedy and not a tragedy,
a farce even, which is why I have given this
scrap of reminiscence a farcical title.*

GRAHAM GREENE

Graham Greene's *May We Borrow
Your Husband?*, adapted for television by Bogarde, opened with
a shot of the husband's
behind while riding in a show-jumping
competition. 'A pretty bum in the saddle,'
was one horsy woman's observation.

The husband was later discovered
honeymooning in Cyprus. The people who
wanted to borrow him were two very camp
interior decorators in search of bric-à-brac
and the gay life. Bogarde played an author
staying at the same hotel.

One of the decorators (David Yelland)
signalled early on that he was also

interested in the author and knew that he
was as gay as he was. The author, eyebrow
raised, clearly indicated he recognised the
signal, but this amusing idea was never
developed; instead the author, not very
believably, fell in love with the incredibly
innocent bride (Charlotte Attenborough)
too naïve to realise her husband was being
seduced.

Bogarde's screenplay took Greene's
short story far too seriously, turning what
was a cynical Somerset Maughamish
comedy of sexual bad manners into a mini-
tragedy of unrequited love. A one-hour
story was strung out to two hours and
snapped long before it was over. His performance, however, was remarkable (as
always) for the range of emotion his face
could convey in close-up without the help
of any dialogue.

The Vision, a television film about the threat of satellite TV, was a big disappointment. It failed to live up to its opening sequence, which promised a satirical exposé of a single information network run by right-wing evangelical Christians, opting instead for science fiction and family melodrama. The television reality would have been so much more interesting.

Bogarde played Gentle Jim, a once famous presenter reduced to appearing in commercials for margarine and opening supermarkets, who is invited to be the frontman for a new People's Channel.

The camera stared long into Bogarde's unbelievably sad face, penetrating a bewilderment, grief and vulnerability, which suited the character perfectly and yet seemed quite separate from it.

The sharpest scene was the one in which Eileen Atkins (in her role of Jim's deceived wife) invited the tabloid press into her living room and strung them a story about her husband being a secret homosexual and having an affair with a communist spy.

directed by
Norman Stone

Lee Remick and
Dirk Bogarde in
The Vision.

CHRONOLOGY

FILM

Release Date	Title	Role	Screenplay	Director
1939	CARRY ON GEORGE	extra	Anthony Kimmins, Leslie Arliss and Val Valentine	Anthony Kimmins
1947	DANCING WITH CRIME	policeman	Brock Williams from original story by Peter Fraser	John Paddy Carstairs
1948	ESTHER WATERS	William Latch	Michael Gordon and William Rose from novel by George Moore	Ian Dalrymple and Peter Proud
	QUARTET	George Bland	R.C. Sherriff based on short story *The Alien Corn* by W. Somerset Maugham	Harold French
	ONCE A JOLLY SWAGMAN	Bill Fox	William Rose and Jack Lee from novel by Montagu Slater	Jack Lee
1949	DEAR MR PROHACK	Charles Prohack	Ian Dalrymple and Donald Bull from novel by Arnold Bennett	Thornton Freeland
	BOYS IN BROWN	Alfie Rawlings	Montgomery Tully based on play by Reginald Beckwith	Montgomery Tully
1950	THE BLUE LAMP	Tom Riley	T.E.B. Clarke additional dialogue by Alexander Mackendrick	Basil Dearden
	SO LONG AT THE FAIR	George Hathaway	Hugh Mills and Anthony Thorne	Terence Fisher and Anthony Darnborough
	THE WOMAN IN QUESTION	Bob Baker	John Cresswell	Anthony Asquith
1951	BLACKMAILED	Stephen Mundy	Hugh Mills and Roger Vadim from novel *Mrs Christopher* by Elizabeth Myers	Marc Allegret
1952	HUNTED	Chris Lloyd	Jack Wittingham	Charles Crichton
	PENNY PRINCESS	Tony Craig	Val Guest	Val Guest
	THE GENTLE GUNMAN	Matt	Roger MacDougall	Basil Dearden
1953	APPOINTMENT IN LONDON	Wing Commander Tim Mason	John Woolridge and Robert Westerby	Philip Leacock
	DESPERATE MOMENT	Simon van Halder	Patrick Kirwan and George H. Brown from novel by Martha Albrand	Compton Bennett
1954	THEY WHO DARE	Lieutenant Graham	Robert Westerby	Lewis Milestone
	DOCTOR IN THE HOUSE	Simon Sparrow	Nicholas Phipps from novel by Richard Gordon	Ralph Thomas
	THE SLEEPING TIGER	Frank Clements	Harold Buchman and Carl Foreman based on novel by Maurice Moiseiwitsch	Joseph Losey
	FOR BETTER FOR WORSE	Tony Howard	based on play by Arthur Watkyn, additional dialogue by Peter Myers and Alec Grahame	J. Lee-Thompson
	THE SEA SHALL NOT HAVE THEM	Flight Sergeant Mackay	Lewis Gilbert and Vernon Harris	Lewis Gilbert
1955	SIMBA	Alan Howard	John Baines, additional dialogue by Robert Estridge, from an original story by Anthony Perry	Brian Desmond Hurst

FILM

FILM

Release Date	Title	Role	Screenplay	Director
1964	HOT ENOUGH FOR JUNE	Nicholas Whistler	Lukas Heller based on novel *Night of Wenceslas* by Lionel Davidson	Ralph Thomas
	KING AND COUNTRY	Captain Hargreaves	Evan Jones from play *Hamp* by John Wilson based on a story by James Lansdale Hodson	Joseph Losey
1965	THE HIGH BRIGHT SUN	Major McGuire	Ian Stuart Black	Ralph Thomas
	DARLING	Robert Gold	Frederick Raphael	John Schlesinger
1966	MODESTY BLAISE	Gabriel	Evan Jones based on *Evening Standard* cartoon-strip created by Peter O'Donnell	Joseph Losey
1967	ACCIDENT	Stephen	Harold Pinter based on novel by Nicholas Mosley	Joseph Losey
	OUR MOTHER'S HOUSE	Charlie Hook	Jeremy Brooks and Haya Harareet based on novel by Julian Gloag	Jack Clayton
1968	SEBASTIAN	Sebastian	Gerald Vaughan-Hughes based on an original screen story by Leo Marks	David Greene
1969	THE FIXER	Bibikov	Dalton Trumbo based on novel by Bernard Malamud	John Frankenheimer
	JUSTINE	Pursewarden	Lawrence B. Marcus based on *The Alexandria Quartet* by Lawrence Durrell	George Cukor
	OH! WHAT A LOVELY WAR	Stephen	Len Deighton from Joan Littlewood stage production based on *The Long Trail* by Charles Chilton	Richard Attenborough
	RETURN TO LOCHABAR	commentary	John Chittock	Don Kelly
1970	LA CADUTA DEGLI DEI (English title: *The Damned*)	Friedrich Bruckmann	Nicola Badalucco, Enrico Medioli and Luchino Visconti	Luchino Visconti
1971	MORTE A VENEZIA (English title: *Death in Venice*)	Gustav von Aschenbach	Luchino Visconti and Nicola Badalucco based on novel by Thomas Mann	Luchino Visconti
1974	THE SERPENT	Philip Boyle	Henri Verneuil and Gilles Perrault based on novel by Pierre Nord	Henri Verneuil
	IL PORTIERE DI NOTTE (English title: *The Night Porter*)	Max	Liliana Cavani and Italo Moscati based on a story by Liliana Cavani, Barbara Alberti and Amedeo Pagani	Liliana Cavani
1975	PERMISSION TO KILL	Alan Curtis	Robert Estridge	Cyril Frankel
1977	PROVIDENCE	Claud Langham	David Mercer	Alain Resnais
	A BRIDGE TOO FAR	Lieutenant General Browning	William Goldman from novel by Cornelius Ryan	Richard Attenborough
1978	DESPAIR	Hermann	Tom Stoppard based on the novel by Vladimir Nabokov	Rainer Werner Fassbinder

THEATRE

MAJOR PRODUCTIONS INCLUDE:

Date	Play	Role	Author	Director	Theatre
1940	CORNELIUS	Lawrence	J.B. Priestley	Henry Cass	Westminster
1941	DIVERSION NO 2 (revue)	various	Herbert Farjeon	Walter Crisham	Wyndham's
	THE GHOST TRAIN		Arnold Ridley	Arnold Ridley	tour
1947	POWER WITHOUT GLORY	Cliff	Michael Clayton Hutton	Chloë Gibson	New Lindsay and Fortune
1948	FOR BETTER FOR WORSE	Tony	Arthur Watkyn	Peter Dearing	Q
1949	FOXHOLE IN THE PARLOUR	Dennis Patterson	Elsa Shelley	Chloë Gibson	New Lindsay
	SLEEP ON MY SHOULDER	Simon	Michael Clayton Hutton	Michael Clayton Hutton	Q
1950	THE SHAUGHRAUN	Captain Molineux	Don Boucicault	Judith Furse	Bedford
	POINT OF DEPARTURE	Orpheus	Jean Anouilh translated by Kitty Black	Peter Ashmore	Lyric, Hammersmith, and Duke of York's
1952	THE VORTEX	Nicky Lancaster	Noël Coward	Michael MacOwan	Lyric, Hammersmith
1955	SUMMERTIME	Alberto	Ugo Betti English version by Henry Reed	Peter Hall	Apollo
1958	JEZABEL	Marc	Jean Anouilh translated by Annabel Maule	Frank Hauser	Playhouse, Oxford

TELEVISION

Date	Play	Role	Author	Director	Company
1947	ROPE	Charles Granillo	Patrick Hamilton	Stephen Harrison	BBC
	POWER WITHOUT GLORY	Cliff	Michael Clayton Hutton	Joel O'Brien	BBC
	THE CASE OF HELVIG DELBO	an underground man	Robert Barr	Robert Barr	BBC
1965	BLITHE SPIRIT	Charles	Noël Coward	George Schaeffer	Hallmark, USA
	THE EPIC THAT NEVER WAS	commentary	Bill Duncalf	Bill Duncalf	BBC
1966	LITTLE MOON OF ALBAN		James Costigan	George Schaeffer	Hallmark, USA
1969	UPON THIS ROCK	Bonnie Prince Charlie	Stanley Abrams	Stanley Abrams	NBC
1981	THE PATRICIA NEAL STORY	Roald Dahl	Robert Anderson from book *Pat and Roald* by Barry Farrell	Anthony Hervey and Anthony Page	CBS
1986	MAY WE BORROW YOUR HUSBAND?	William	Graham Greene adapted by Dirk Bogarde	Bob Mahoney	Yorkshire
1988	THE VISION	James Marriner	William Nicholson	Norman Stone	BBC

ACKNOWLEDGEMENTS

The author would like to begin by thanking Yvonne McFarlane, Frank Phillips and Rachel Gosling of Ebury Press and his designer Roger Daniels.

The author and publisher would like to express their appreciation to the following for their assistance and/or permission to reproduce the photographs. Every effort has been made to trace the copyright owners.

Action Films, 175, 176, 177; Bavaria Film Studios, 181, 182, 183; copyright BBC (Enterprises), 185; BBC Hulton Picture Library, 25; La Boetie Films, 167; Columbia Pictures Corporation, 92, 94, 95, 106, 108, 109; Eros Films Ltd, 57, 64, 65; London Independent Producers, 140, 142, 143, 144, 145; Lotar Films, 168, 169, 170, 171; Angus McBean courtesy Harvard Theatre Collection, 16, 34, 35, 42, 43; Metro-Goldwyn-Mayer, 85, 86, 87, 88, 89, 90, 91, 100, 110, 111, 146, 147, 148, 149, 153; The National Film Archive London, 7, 11, 19, 20, 21, 22, 23, 24, 26, 27, 28, 31, 32, 33, 36, 37, 38, 39, 40, 46, 47, 48, 51, 52, 53, 54, 56, 57, 60, 61, 62, 63, 64, 65, 67, 68, 71, 73, 74, 75, 77, 81, 82, 85, 86, 87, 96, 97, 98, 99, 101, 103, 104, 105, 106, 108, 109, 110, 113, 114, 116, 117, 118, 123, 127, 129, 132, 133, 134, 135, 140, 142, 143, 145, 150, 153, 154, 156, 157, 158, 159, 163, 164, 165, 167, 169, 175, 176, 177, 179, 181, 182; Paramount Pictures, 150, 151, 156; The Rank Organisation plc, 1, 18, 19, 20, 21, 22, 23, 24, 26, 27, 28, 30, 31, 32, 33, 36, 37, 38, 39, 40, 41, 44, 45, 47, 51, 52, 53, 58, 60, 61, 62, 63, 67, 68, 69, 71, 72, 73, 74, 75, 76, 77, 78, 79, 81, 82, 96, 97, 98, 99, 101, 103, 104, 105, 117, 124, 125, 130, 131; Twentieth Century-Fox, 136, 138, 139, 154, 155; The Times Newspapers Limited, 15, 17, 83; United Artists, 114, 115, 116, 179; Warner Bros, 2, 161, 163, 164, 165, 172, 173; Warner-Pathé, 112, 113, 118, 120, 121, 122, 123, 127, 128, 129, 132, 133, 134, 135, 157, 158, 159; Weintraub Entertainment Group, 46, 48, 49, 54, 55, 56; Yorkshire Television Ltd, 184.

The author would like to add a personal note of thanks to Anita Appel, Brian Baxter, Sheila Formoy and H.M. Tennent Ltd, Catherine Johnson, Alison Rogers, Simon Scott, and everybody at the BFI in the reference library, stills library and viewing facilities.

INDEX